727094   12431A

AUSTRALIA
A LUCKY LAND

DISCOVERING our HERITAGE

by Al Stark

𝒹P DILLON PRESS, INC.
Minneapolis, Minnesota 55415

Photographic Acknowledgments

Photographs have been reproduced through the courtesy of Al Stark and the Detroit News, *and Milt and Joan Mann of Cameramann International Ltd. (© 1987, pages 8, 18, 58, 94-95, 98, 106). Special thanks to Promotion Australia.*

Library of Congress Cataloging in Publication Data

Stark, Al.
   Australia, a lucky land.

   (Discovering our heritage)
   Bibliography: p.
   Includes index.
   Summary: Describes the people, culture, geography, history, and customs of "the land down under."
   1. Australia—Juvenile literature. [1. Australia] I. Title. II. Series.
DU96.S73   1987   994   87-13424
ISBN 0-87518-365-4

Dillon Press, Inc., 242 Portland Avenue South
Minneapolis, Minnesota 55415

Printed in the United States of America
      4 5 6 7 8 9 10 96 95 94 93 92 91 90 89

Contents

Fast Facts About Australia   4

Map of Australia   6

1   The Land Down Under   9

2   The Colorful Aussies 30

3   The British Go Ashore 42

4   Independence At Last 61

5   The Natural Australia 69

6   Australia Celebrates 83

7   All the Comforts of Home 93

8   The Australian Classroom 112

9   Sports Under the Sun 122

10   Aussies Abroad 134

Appendix A: Australian Slang 144

Appendix B: Consulates and Embassies
             in the United States
             and Canada 146

Selected Bibliography 148

Index 149

Fast Facts About Australia

Official Name: *Commonwealth of Australia.*

Capital: Canberra.

Location: Southeast of mainland Asia. The island of Australia lies between the Indian Ocean to the west and the South Pacific to the east.

Area: 2,966,150 square miles (7,682,300 square kilometers). *Greatest Distances*: north-south—1,950 miles (3,138 kilometers); east-west—2,475 miles (3,983 kilometers). *Coastlines*: 17,366 miles (27,948 square kilometers), including 779 miles (1,254 kilometers) for Tasmania and 510 miles (821 kilometers) for offshore islands.

Elevation: *Highest*—Mount Kosciusko, 7,310 feet (2,228 meters) above sea level. *Lowest*—Lake Eyre 52 feet (16 meters) below sea level.

Population: 16,102,000 (1987 estimate). *Distribution*—87 percent urban, 13 percent rural. *Density*—5 persons per square mile (2 persons per square kilometer).

Form of Government: Constitutional monarchy. Queen Elizabeth II of Great Britain is the head of state, and a prime minister is the head of the government.

Important Products: *Agriculture*—sheep, wool, cattle,

dairy products, wheat, sugarcane, fruits, barley. *Manufacturing*—processed foods; iron, steel, and other metals; transportation equipment; paper; household appliances. *Mining*—bauxite, coal, copper, gold, iron ore, lead, manganese, natural gas, nickel, opals, petroleum, silver, tin, tungsten, uranium, zinc.

Basic Unit of Money: Australian dollar.

Official Language: English.

Major Religions: Church of England, Roman Catholic.

Flag: Australia's flag has a dark blue background. In the upper left corner is a red-and-white British Union Flag. Below is a large white star for the Commonwealth. To the right are five white stars for the constellation Southern Cross.

National Anthems: *Advance Australia Fair* (national); *God Save the Queen* (royal).

Major Holidays: New Year's Day—January 1; Australia Day—January 26; Good Friday, Easter Sunday, Easter Monday (dates vary), ANZAC Day—April 25; Commonwealth Day—May 24; Christmas Day—December 25; Boxing Day—December 26.

NEW GUINEA

Coral Sea

GREAT BARRIER REEF

CAPE YORK PENINSULA

Cairns

GREAT BARRIER REEF

ERRITORY

A L I A

AGES

lice Springs

SIMPSON DESERT

QUEENSLAND

PACIFIC

OCEAN

AUSTRALIA

Brisbane

Darling River

NEW SOUTH WALES

Bathurst
Sydney SYDNEY HARBOR
BOTANY BAY

Adelaide

Murray

Canberra ★

River

AUSTRALIAN
CAPITAL
TERRITORY

VICTORIA

SNOWY MTS

**Mount
Kosciusko**

Melbourne

AUSTRALIAN ALPS

Tasman

Sea

TASMANIA

Hobart

1. The Land Down Under

"G'day, mate!"

This is the famous greeting of Australia, and all by itself it says a lot about the land and the people Down Under. The greeting is informal and friendly, and Australia is both of these.

"Mate" does not mean a sailor or one's spouse. It means "my special friend," and it is a very important word among Australians. In the harsh, forbidding interior of Australia, in the early days and even now, it is very important to have a companion on whom one can rely. Life can depend on it. People work together or all suffer.

In Australia, these good friends who will stand by each other no matter what are called mates. Even in the modern and sophisticated Australia of the 1980s, "mateship" is very important.

So when someone says to us, "G'day, mate," it means they expect we will be friends. They are willing to accept us as we are, if we will accept them in the same way. This is exactly the manner in which Australians make visitors and travelers welcome, and it helps explain why Australians have so many friends around the world. Most Australians are lively and open people who enjoy

An Australian "cowboy" checks the cattle at a water hole in Silver Pines station in the Outback.

life and good times, and they are very easy to like. Australians look around them and they like what they see. They call Australia the "Lucky Country," and they mean it.

The Island Itself

Australia, the only continent that is also an island, lies well south of the equator at the far western edge of the Pacific Ocean. Its eastern coasts are washed by the South Pacific, and its western and southern coasts by the Indian Ocean. Australia got the nickname "Down Under" in the days when many homes and every classroom had a globe. Since the continent was down at the bottom of the globe, American and British people, located up toward the top, began to refer to Australia as Down Under. The island is about 7,500 miles (12,000 kilometers) southwest of Los Angeles. By airplane it takes about thirteen hours to get from Southern California to Australia.

Australia is an enormous country, covering almost 3 million square miles (almost 8 million square kilometers) in all. This makes it just a little bit smaller than the United States. Yet, where the population of the United States is more than 200 million, Australia's is just over 16 million. Australia is the least-populated continent in the world.

The British Link

Because Australia was settled by the British, English is the official language of the country. Another of Australia's links with England is religion. But religion for most Australians plays a minor role in day-to-day life. Formally, 36 percent of the population is Anglican, or Church of England, which is the official state church of England. Other Protestant groups make up about 25 percent of the population, and 33 percent is Roman Catholic. The Australian Constitution forbids a state religion and guarantees religious freedom. Because of this, most of the world's religions are represented in Australia.

Australia is the only continent that is all under one government, and is formally known as the Commonwealth of Australia. Once ruled as a British colony, Australia's government is still tied to that of Great Britain. Great Britain's monarch, Queen Elizabeth II, is also queen of Australia and its official head of state, but she has very little power in the Australian government. Her main purpose is to serve as a symbol of the historic tie between the two countries.

Officially, the federal government of Australia is headed by a governor general, who represents the queen. But like the queen's, the governor general's role is mainly symbolic.

Australia has a parliamentary system of government and a prime minister to run its day-to-day affairs. The Federal Parliament is the main governing body. Like the United States Congress, it has an upper house called the Senate and a lower house called the House of Representatives. Bills become law after they are passed by both houses of Parliament. The prime minister is the leader of the political party or the coalition (combination) of parties with the majority of seats in the House of Representatives.

Since World War II, Australia's government has been most often conservative. On the present-day political scene, three political parties are dominant. The Australian Labor party, the Liberal party, and the National party which represents farmers and rural Australians.

Australia's Liberal party and its Labor party have both had their turns in office. The Liberal party is actually the more conservative party, and the Labor party is made up of liberals with a strong labor backing. In 1983 the Labor party gained power and Robert (Bob) Hawke, a union man, became prime minister.

Australian States

Australia has six states. The five on the mainland are New South Wales, Victoria, South Australia, Western

The prime minister of Australia, Robert Hawke, was elected for the third time in 1987.

Australia, and Queensland. The sixth state is the island of Tasmania, off the southern coast. The Northern Territory has the special status of a self-governing territory. The federal government administers the Australian Capital Territory (similar to the District of Columbia in the United States), where the capital Canberra is located.

The states and the Northern Territory each have their own regional governments and streaks of independence. However, because almost all authority to tax in Australia is reserved for the federal government, the states aren't as independent as they like to say they are.

Each state has its own capital, which functions not only as the state's political center but as its commercial, industrial, and cultural center as well. Sydney, a wonderfully lively city, is the capital of New South Wales and is Australia's largest city. Melbourne, state capital of Victoria, is elegant and dignified and hosted the 1956 Olympics. Adelaide, a lovely, quiet city, is capital of South Australia; and Perth, host for the America's Cup sailing races for four years, is the capital of Western Australia. In the Northern Territory, Darwin is the capital and in Queensland, it is Brisbane. Tasmania's capital is Hobart.

Each of these cities is located near natural harbors on the seacoast. The coastal strip on the southern and eastern edges of Australia has been called one of the nicest locations in all the world to live. It is cooled by the sea breeze in the summer; the winters are mild; and the rain keeps things green throughout the year. This temperate strip runs from above Brisbane on the eastern coast of Australia around to Adelaide on the southern coast. Almost three-fourths of Australia's population lives in this area.

The Great Empty

The rest of Australia is sparsely populated because most of the country's interior is desert or near-desert. Australia is the driest continent on earth. The government acknowledges that much of the interior is unlivable, and travelers can discover that for themselves. It is possible to drive all day long in the dry interior deserts of Australia and see no living creature except for sheep and kangaroo.

Australia is also the flattest continent, though it does have some mountain ranges. In the southeastern corner of the country are the Australian Alps, which consist of several ranges. The Snowy Mountains are the best known of these, and Australia's highest peak, Mount Kosciusko, is located here. In the winter, many of the Snowy Mountains' peaks are covered with snow, which makes the area popular among skiers.

In Central Australia rise the MacDonnell and Musgrave Ranges, but these are much lower in elevation than the Australian Alps. South of the MacDonnell Range is

Skiers enjoy the snowfields at Smigging Holes on Mount Kosciusko in New South Wales.

Ayers Rock. Every year, hundreds of tourists journey into the desert to see this giant stone hill. Ayers Rock is about 1,000 feet (300 meters) high and over 1.5 miles (2.4 kilometers) long! Except for these few mountain ranges, much of Australia, especially its interior, resembles a table top.

The interior of Australia is known as the Outback, famous the world over as one of the great rugged fron-

Ayers Rock, in the heart of the Red Center of Australia, is probably the nation's best-known natural tourist attraction.

tiers. The interior is also home to one of the most fascinating ethnic peoples anywhere, the Australian Aborigines. For thousands of years, these tribes lived in the harsh desert, struggling for survival. The ancestors of today's Aborigines were the first inhabitants of Australia. Since the arrival of white settlers, their history has been similar to that of American Indians in the United States.

The red sands of the Simpson Desert show why the Australian desert is called the Red Center.

Australians, who have a rich way with slang, have other names besides the Outback for their strange, hard, and unfriendly middle country. Some simply call it "Beyond." Others call it "Beyond Beyond." Four great deserts—the Simpson Desert, the Great Sandy Desert, the Gibson Desert, and the Great Victoria Desert—come together in the almost exact geographic center of Australia. This area is commonly known as the "Red Center," because the rocks and sand are reddish in color.

Some Australians simply refer to everything any distance from the coast as the "Great Empty," and let the name-calling go at that.

As you travel inland from the sea, no matter where on the coast you start, you will pass through miles and miles of scrubland. Here, the grass is sparse, and the trees low and weak-looking. After this scrubland comes the desert, the really empty part of Australia. If you look at a map of the Outback, you might be surprised to see that rivers run through it and that the region is dotted with lakes. But these are almost always dry, sometimes for years at a time. There is one Outback lake called Lake Disappointment, and its name tells its story.

Because Australia is in the Southern Hemisphere, winter occurs in July and August, the reverse of North America and Europe. Spring rains come in September and October. Sometimes the rain comes in torrents, and the Outback's many dry rivers and lakes flood madly. Sometimes the rain is only a few drops that kick up dust.

In the Australian summer, November to February, temperatures in the Outback quite commonly reach 130 to 140 degrees Fahrenheit (54 to 60 degrees Celsius). In this terrible heat everything shimmers and seems to constantly change shape. The few trees in the deep Outback have had to struggle in their parched climate to survive. Their branches tend to be twisted and bent, as if the fight has deformed them.

Australia's Gold

As strangely empty as it is, the Outback is the source of much of Australia's wealth. The land gave up gold to the people brave and strong enough to explore it in the early days, and its surviving mines still produce gold in large quantities. In a couple of places, the Outback is rich in opals, those milky jewels carrying streaks of fire. Nearly all of the world's top-quality opals come from Australia, from diggings near tiny towns such as Lightning Ridge in New South Wales and Coober Pedy in South Australia. There are important diamond and silver mines in the Outback, as well as considerable reserves of less glamorous resources such as copper, iron ore, lead, manganese, nickel, tin, and zinc. Australia is a major supplier of coal to countries like Japan and leads the world in the production of bauxite, the ore from which aluminum is made. There are large deposits of uranium, a radioactive element used in nuclear weapons and fuel, especially in the Northern Territory. For political reasons, much of the uranium is not mined.

Along with mining, farming is a very important element in Australia's economy. Farmers in Western Australia, particularly, grow immense crops of wheat that they market around the world. Queensland also produces wheat in large quantities. In the parts of the state where the climate is almost tropical (the northern

These merino rams (male sheep) are herded together at a stud ranch in Western Australia.

coastal area around Cairns) grow vast quantities of sugarcane, which is also exported.

All over the Outback, except in the driest deserts, roam the sheep. Wool from the merino sheep gave the country its first real economy and Australia still produces 35 percent of the world's wool. Australia has about nine sheep for every person. Everyone thinks of the kangaroo or the cuddly koala when they think of Aus-

Australia is famous for its stretches of beautiful coastline. This is a crowded city beach at Newcastle in New South Wales.

tralia, but actually the sheep is by far the most important animal in Australia's history.

Coastal Cities

The wealth of the Outback flows through the cities on the coast. Sydney, located in the southeast of the country on what is perhaps the most beautiful harbor in the world, is Australia's main center of business, finance, and the arts. Metropolitan Sydney spreads north and south along the Pacific Ocean coast and inland about fifty miles (eighty kilometers) to the Blue Mountains, a natural barrier.

Nearly a quarter of all Australians live in greater Sydney. Its population totals more than three million and is still growing. Sydney is home to one of the wonders of the twentieth century, the magnificent seashell-shaped building that is the Sydney Opera House (see pages 84, 91, 94-95). The inhabitants of Sydney come from almost every part of the world, and the variety of people gives the city great energy.

Melbourne, south and west of Sydney, is a little more conservative. It is a city of old wealth and commerce, more stately than the bubbly Sydney. The second largest city, Melbourne is home to just under three million residents.

Adelaide, from which some of the important explorations were launched in the early days, has about one million inhabitants. It may be the prettiest Australian city of them all. Close to the sea, it is bordered on one side by the Adelaide Hills, where many people live up above the city proper. Adelaide's city center is surrounded by a broad greenbelt of parks, playing fields, and nature trails. This greenbelt gives it a calm, restful atmosphere.

The Murray River, Australia's longest permanently

flowing river, empties into the ocean southeast of Adelaide. The Murray starts in the Snowy Mountains and winds westward about 1,600 miles (2,576 kilometers) before reaching the sea. Along the way, it is fed by the country's longest river, the Darling. The Darling River begins in central New South Wales and flows southwestward about 1,700 miles (2,737 kilometers) before joining the Murray. The Darling is dry in the winter. For most of the river's length, however, its flow is greater in the summer with increased rainfall in its area. Thus, when most of the other southern rivers dry up, the Darling still supplies water to the Murray.

Perth is on the Indian Ocean, far to the west of Sydney and the other large cities. Yet, ever since a yacht from the Royal Perth Yacht Club stunned the world by winning the America's Cup from the United States in 1983, Perth has felt directly at the center of things Australian. An enormous amount of attention has been focused on Perth since that yacht race, and hundreds of millions of dollars of new construction has taken place there. The city is booming and the one million people who live there are proud of its progress.

Darwin, capital of the Northern Territory, is far removed from everyplace else on the other side of the vast Outback. Only about 65,000 people live there. It is the part of Australia closest to Asia and Indonesia, and it has sizable communities from both places. Darwin is well within the steamy tropics. To combat the heat, the hotel rooms have fans on the ceilings and the men wear walking shorts rather than trousers.

Brisbane, halfway up the eastern coast, has a population of about 1,200,000. It is a country town that has grown and grown, but has never lost its small town feel. Its tropical climate makes Queensland a favorite winter vacation place for Australians, much as Florida is the warm weather getaway for many Americans in the winter.

Hobart, on the island state of Tasmania, is a city of just under 200,000 people. Tasmania is a rugged place. Because it is the part of Australia closest to Antarctica, it is just about the only place in the country where a person can expect it to get really cold in the winter.

The federal government is located at Canberra, the only major Australian city not on a seacoast. Both Sydney and Melbourne wanted to be the site of the federal capital, and a political disagreement developed. The solution finally reached in 1913 was to locate the capital halfway between the two rival cities, creating a new city. It was named Canberra, an Aboriginal word meaning "meeting place." The capital is part of neither state; instead it is part of the Australian Capital Territory. Canberra has about 250,000 residents, many of them government employees. The city plans were drawn by an American architect, Walter Burley Griffin, and so

Canberra's general design resembles that of our District of Columbia.

Beaches and the Great Barrier Reef

Australia is blessed with endless beaches, wide and sandy, and every state boasts about its shoreline. Queensland not only has beautiful beaches, but it has the one great natural wonder in Australia, the Great Barrier Reef. The Great Barrier Reef hugs the Pacific coast of the continent and runs from Bundaberg, just north of Brisbane, all the way to New Guinea, a distance of 1,200 miles (1,932 kilometers).

The reef is a living thing, made up of layers and layers of coral polyps, which are tiny shelled sea animals. The brightly colored reef is home to 300 varieties of coral, from blue to shades of pink and purple. There are, by best count, 1,400 varieties of fish living around the reef, and they are as colorful as the corals. In season, great gamefish, notably marlin, gather off the reef, and anglers come from all over the world to fish for them. Other vacationers enjoy the reef as well and there are many island resorts nearby to host them. Travelers dive at the reef, walk it in low tide, and fly over it in special aircraft. In 1979, Australia created the Great Barrier Reef Marine Park, with its research center and bird sanctuary.

More and more Americans are going Down Under

In this aerial view of the Great Barrier Reef, parts of the long reef chain rise up through the clear blue water.

on vacation to see Australia for themselves, and many American firms are represented there, too. Qantas Airways Limited, Australia's only international airline, connects the continent with all the world. Many Australians have traveled to America and Europe, where they have distinguished themselves against all competition in the arts, popular entertainment, science, and sports.

Australia has opened its doors not only to travelers, but also to emigrants from much of the world. Today Australia has a richly diverse population made up of many nationalities. A number of European countries other than England have helped populate Australia, including Ireland, Italy, Greece, Yugoslavia, West Germany, and the Netherlands. In addition, Australia has made itself something of a haven for people from the troubled spots of the world. Since World War II it has taken in many people from Eastern Europe. Lately it has become the new home of people from the war-torn areas of the Middle East and Southeast Asia.

Though this friendly country welcomes thousands each year, it sometimes seems to ignore the problems of its people. More and more Australian children fail to complete their education, and many face an uncertain future. Australia also wrestles with its Aborigine problem, never quite understanding the difficulties that its native Australians face. This situation is disturbing, because many Aborigines live in poverty on the fringes of Australian society.

Although Australia enjoys a generally high standard of living, the government now spends one quarter of its national budget on welfare aid for the poor. Some of Australia's leaders worry about the economy and question whether it will continue to support the comfortable lifestyle of most people.

But for the most part, there is little worry evident among the people of Australia. Relaxed and friendly, they are confident about their future.

2. The Colorful Aussies

The Aussie character would be difficult to pinpoint because of the great variety in Australia's people. The culture has become a blend of a strong British heritage, the huge number of immigrants that flooded the continent after World War II, and the Australian Aborigines.

But if one thing distinguishes the Australian character and personality it is the Aussie's streak of independence. Australians prize their individual freedoms and they believe that one person's opinions are as important as another's, even when one is a bishop and the other is a baker. Although they elect leaders, they are distrustful of authority if it is too heavy-handed. Given a choice, they tend to side with the little man or woman—the underdog.

These national traits could date back to the early days of the country's settlement. Most of the first white Australians were convicts from England, some convicted with good reason and some imprisoned unfairly. For many of them, being transported to Australia provided a new chance at life, and they were determined never to be locked up or hemmed in again. Those who had been jailed without just cause found it hard to trust

An Outback sheep rancher north of New South Wales adjusts some feed pails.

authority ever again, wherever they found themselves.

Another factor in the development of the Australian character was Australia itself. In this vast, new country, those who wanted room where they could live with no bosses but themselves, could find it. It is no surprise that the Outback, that immense, empty space, has had such a great influence on the Australian personality. Australians admire the men and women who pushed into the interior—the swagmen, the sheep ranchers, and even the lawbreaking bushrangers—and have inherited many character traits and attitudes from them.

Slang, Australia-Style

Australians have a gift for the sarcastic remark, particularly when they think people are making too much of themselves. Often the tart remarks are delivered in a rich and earthy slang, famous the world over.

This colorful language is spoken with the Aussie version of an English accent that has a flavor all its own. In Australia, "day" sounds like "die," and "prime minister" sounds like "prymista." Some think the slang was started by ex-convicts who purposely mangled proper English as a way of thumbing their noses at an England that had the nerve to put them in prison. There is no limit to what Australians can do with slang. For instance, "have a Captain Cook" means "have a look." A policeman is a "walloper," and a busybody is a "sticky-beak." A "silvertail" is someone who thinks he or she is better than anyone else. Australian slang is easy once you get the swing of it, and it is fun.

The Wandering Swagmen

Of all the Australians who have been celebrated in story and song, none is more famous than the swagman.

He carried his belongings in a roll on his back. That was his swag. From this roll or from his belt hung a tin cup, which he used as a pot to boil water for his tea. He would tie small corks to the brim of his hat like a fringe. When the flies and gnats that swarm through the Outback got too thick about his face, he would simply give his head an energetic shake and the corks would dance, shooing the flies away.

Particularly in the early days when there were no vehicles, swagmen walked wherever they went, sometimes for tremendous distances, sometimes from one coast to another. They slept outside most of the time and they ate whatever they could fish out of the water holes or hunt down along the way.

Many of them had no real home. They lived wherever they were. Although they might pair up if they met someone they didn't mind traveling with, each was on his own and each followed his own direction. Some used only first names. Some used nicknames and never told anyone who they really were.

Some swagmen were never anything but tramps, who thieved what they could. They had been pickpockets and cutpurses in England and they never changed their ways. The well-known song, "Waltzing Matilda," tells the story of a swagman who drowns trying to get away with a sheep he has stolen.

But many of the swagmen were skilled at some

trade, or at least handy. Among these were men who had never been real criminals, but who had been imprisoned in England because they owed debts they could not pay. When they went into the Outback, they were able to find work whenever they wanted it. The sheep ranchers could always use another hand, particularly one who might be able to repair equipment or work with animals. As settlement spread inland, common trails developed. These usually led from one isolated sheep station to another—through tiny Outback towns, past water holes, and past scrub forests where game might be found. The feet of the swagmen helped smooth out these trails, which became Australia's first rough roads.

A swagman might make his way across the entire country on these trails, stopping at a ranch or farm to work a few months, then moving on to the next one. Even if there was no work for him, he was welcome to stay for a meal and sleep in the bunkhouse.

A common code grew up in the Outback. No traveler was refused food or shelter. The Outback was hard and dangerous. Everyone helped everyone else, because people understood that their own lives might one day depend on the assistance of another. When the settlers finally built towns in the Outback, it became a rule at the hotels that anyone who walked into town ate and drank free. Anyone who rode in or arrived in a vehicle had to pay—and pay a very steep price.

Tony Mortress is the modern version of Australia's famous Outback wanderers. Now a ranger in Kakadu National Park, he has moved around the country from job to job. He has been a guide, miner, and camp assistant since he left high school.

Above all, the swagmen were free and beholden to no one, wandering wherever they wished, wherever their feet led them. Australia's enormous open spaces gave them plenty of room and they took advantage of it.

There is still a lot of room to roam in Australia, and the spirit of the swagman is still alive. Even in today's Australia it is not at all uncommon to meet carpenters or bricklayers who have worked in every state of the country, just moving around as the whim strikes them. Nor is it unusual to find a park ranger who, since finishing high school, has been a gold miner, a sheepherder, a camp guide, and an opal miner, just for the enjoyment of trying new things and seeing new places.

Gold and the Bushrangers

The Outback always meant hard work. In 1851 gold was discovered near Bathurst on the Macquarie River, about two hundred miles (about three hundred kilometers) west of Sydney. For the people who rushed to the gold fields, hard work began to mean a chance for a big payoff or maybe even a fortune. That possibility also attracted robbers, who in the early days of Australia were called bushrangers.

The most famous bushranger of all was Ned Kelly, who was born during the early 1850s in northern Victoria to Irish immigrant parents. Kelly, by all the evidence, was nothing but a thief and a killer, but he benefited from Australia's great affection for the underdog in any argument against authority.

Gold meant wealth. Wealth often meant big business and big banks. It was almost guaranteed that anyone who picked the pockets of the wealthy by robbing their gold wagons would become something of a hero to the working classes, whose lives were often made up of endless dull labor and who didn't like the upper classes much anyway. Kelly was a clever outlaw who sometimes took whole towns hostage. He portrayed himself as a Robin Hood and he had many fans. Songs were written about him, and they are still sung. But he over-reached himself finally and was captured and hanged, when he was just twenty-six years old.

The Working People

Today, Australians still believe in equality. Wealth does not define people by class. Most Australians consider themselves to be members of the middle class, which holds the same general values of middle classes everywhere. It prizes good conduct, order, and public safety. The middle class pays taxes to provide modern police forces, and it likes to see its police on the job. But every once in a while a police department in modern Australia will complain that it is not getting cooperation from the public. When that happens, someone always remarks that this is a throwback to the attitudes of the earliest white Australians, who were suspicious of law enforcement officers and frequently sided with those the officers were after.

Traditionally labor unions have been very strong in Australia. This also began during the country's early days through the experiences of the swagmen. If they didn't like the work they were asked to do on one sheep station, they'd quit and go to another. Station owners and foremen quickly learned to make sure that their hands agreed with the work scheduled for the day. This was a measure of self-protection. If a sheep station's workers marched off just at shearing time, a year's work and profit might be lost.

Business owners from England who came to Australia in the 1800s were amazed when they listened to a ranch foreman or a mining boss consulting with workers about what should be done instead of ordering them to do this or that. This was long before industrial labor unions, and it was unheard of in the mills and on farms of Europe. But it was already the Australian way.

Today there is ample evidence of the strength of modern labor unions, and of Australia's continuing respect for the effort of working people. Australians are protected in illness, unemployment, injury, and old age by a broad selection of government programs. Most working Australians get four weeks vacation and many get six, all of it paid and with a vacation bonus on top.

Every now and then some critic says that it is too easy for working people in Australia. These critics worry that if life is too easy, the country may fall behind other nations in a world where change follows change. But most Australians work just as hard as anyone else. It took effort, skill, and brains to build cities as splendid as Australia's. Making a living in the Outback took grinding, brave effort, and determination. Everywhere you look in Australia, you see the rewards of hard work.

The Flood of Immigrants

A very rich influence on the national character and personality has come from abroad—from the great number of immigrants who have been welcomed to Australia since World War II ended in 1945. Roughly four million people from 120 other countries have settled in Australia since the war. England continues to contribute more new Australians than any other country, and the rest of Europe—particularly Greece and Italy—also contributes a significant number. But people from Asia and Oceania, the vast Pacific with all its islands, are also sending so many people to Australia that in real ways they are changing the look and flavor of the country.

Many new Australians have had to learn English, and many have had to struggle to fit into the country's society. But, all in all, their transformation into Australians has been without particular conflict. They have enriched Australia with their own cultures and viewpoints.

The Aborigines

The Aborigines lived in Australia long before the white people came, but they have little influence on the

national character of the country as it is today. From the time the first white settlers landed in the late eighteenth century, Aborigines were pushed to the side of things. In the two hundred years since, they have never gained a place in the Australian mainstream.

Whites have a fascination with the Aborigines' ability to survive in the worst parts of the interior. Aborigines are regarded as masters at tracking others in the wastelands of the Outback, and even today they are asked to help when a child, camper, or adventurer is lost in the wilderness. But they are only called when all else has failed.

Today there are about 165,000 Aborigines left in Australia, making up about 1 percent of the population. They are too few to have political power, except as scars on Australia's conscience. The bush life no longer is appealing to young Aborigines who have seen cars and movies and have eaten at McDonald's. Yet far too many of them drop out of school, which means that few are able to hold better than low-paying jobs. Many young Aborigines are idle, and many get into trouble. The great majority of Aboriginal families live on welfare.

The many different kinds of people that now live in Australia have changed the once very British flavor of the country into a rich cultural blend. All the people of Australia seem to share a love of their land, its open spaces, its wonderful climate, and its sense of freedom.

A pet possum sits on the head of a fourteen-year-old Aborigine girl from the Tiwi tribe of Bathurst Island.

3. *The British Go Ashore*

Before 1788, when the white settlers arrived, 300,000 to 350,000 Aborigines had all of Australia to themselves. Australia was practically empty. The Aborigines were immigrants, in the best opinion of scholars. It is believed that they were originally Southeast Asian people who migrated by choice or were driven by force to what we know as Australia. They came by boat or traveled on foot over the land bridges that once connected Australia to New Guinea and Asia. When the seas rose, the land bridges disappeared under water, and Australia was left an island. No one knows who may have been living in Australia when the Aborigines arrived.

In Australia, it is estimated that there were about five hundred separate tribes of Aborigines. The tribes were most commonly organized along family lines, and many tribes were quite small.

To the best of anyone's knowledge, a single Aboriginal nation never existed in Australia. Although tribes had contact with each other, sometimes friendly and sometimes hostile, each kept itself separate from the others. Some tribes lived in the deserts, others near the coasts. Each had its own traditional area, but all moved from place to place within their areas as the seasons changed. They built no permanent settlements or villages.

The most desirable locations for tribes to live were those along the few rivers in Australia that could be counted on to have water in them. Living was easier where there was a dependable water supply. More plants grew there, animals would come to the river, and fish swam in its water. When tribes fought each other, it was often over rights to the best-watered camping grounds along the rivers. Wherever they lived, Aborigines were hunters and gatherers. They didn't plant crops or raise animals for food.

The land was life to the Aborigines, and it was of the highest importance in their spiritual lives. Most believed in what they call the Dreaming, when the spirits shaped the world and gave it life. The spirits then went to live in a particular tree or a particular rock. These trees and rocks became sacred to the Aborigines, to be honored, preserved, and safeguarded. Ayers Rock is one of these sacred Aboriginal spots.

Although one tribe of Aborigines might have fought another over a particularly fertile and game-filled piece of land, most believed the earth did not belong to any one person, but belonged to all. The berries on a bush belonged to the people who happened to come across them. No one's permission was needed to eat them. They were a gift from the earth. They felt the same way about

Aborigines hunted turtles on the islands of the Great Barrier Reef.
They drew pictures on cave walls such as this one.

game. Any animal or fish belonged to the man who
could catch it.

Aborigines often painted elaborate designs of human and animal figures in caves or on rocks and bark.
Some Aborigines carved figures from wood or stone and
then painted them. Others wove beautiful baskets, mats,
and bags. Today, many Aboriginal paintings are col-
lected, and wall paintings are protected by the law.

It is estimated that the Aborigines had Australia to

themselves for thirty-five or forty thousand years. During this time, they had no idea there was a place called Europe where white people had learned to build sailing ships that could carry them across the seas to many strange and different places.

On the Map

Australia first appeared on maps drawn in Europe in about 1500. Early Chinese and Arab voyagers talked of a great southern land east of India, and their tales were carried back to Europe. The earliest maps only guessed at where Australia was and what it looked like. No one knew it was surrounded by water; they assumed it was attached to Antarctica.

Mapmakers named this mysterious place in Latin, calling it *Terra Australis Incognita. Terra* means land; *australis* means southern; and *incognita* means unknown —the Unknown Southern Land. The greatest exploring nations of Europe, in the first flush of their seagoing power, all hunted for Australia.

Some historians think the Portuguese were already familiar with Australia's eastern coast in the fifteenth century, although for reasons unknown they neither announced it nor tried to settle there. In 1606 another Portuguese, Luis Vaez de Torres, sailed along the southern coast of New Guinea, in the narrow strait that separates it from Australia's northern coast. Torres gave his name to the strait, but as far as anyone knows he sailed through it without catching sight of Australia.

The Dutch did better. Willem Jansz, sailing from Java in Indonesia, landed on the western shore of the Cape York Peninsula, at the far northeastern tip of Australia. He is regarded as the first European known to have set foot on the continent. He decided the prospects for treasure or settlement were poor, and he found the natives unfriendly. He reported to his superiors that he found no good reason to stay or settle. Over the next thirty-five years other Dutch explorers came to the coast, mostly by accident, having been blown off course. None of them reported anything more encouraging than Jansz had. The Dutch decided this could not be the Unknown Southern Land that the Chinese and Arabs had talked of, and they continued to look elsewhere.

In 1642 the Dutch sent Abel Tasman out to look again. He found Tasmania, which he called Van Dieman's Land, and he also discovered New Zealand and the islands of Fiji. The Tasman Sea, which separates Australia and New Zealand, is named for him.

The first British sailor known to have landed in Australia was William Dampier, a part-time explorer and a part-time pirate. Dampier scouted the west coast and went ashore at King Sound in 1688. He was as discouraged as Jansz had been. He sailed off, firmly believing

Captain James Cook.

that it would be a waste of time to seek trade or gold there.

Australia lay undisturbed for almost another century. On April 28, 1770, Captain James Cook, on his way back to England after a long voyage, steered his ship into a natural harbor just south of present-day Sydney on the Pacific coast. Cook carried two famous botanists with him who went ashore and brought back to the ship many

unusual specimens of animal, plant, and bird life. Seeing
how excited the botanists were at their discoveries, Cook
decided to name the bay where his ship was anchored
Botany Bay.

Cook and his crew stayed in Australian waters until
August, making their way up the entire coast as far as the
tip of Cape York Peninsula. Before sailing for home,
Cook claimed the eastern half of Australia for the King
of England. In London, he reported that although he
had gone ashore at Botany Bay, he did not think this was
the sought-after Terra Australis Incognita. He thought it
was part of New Holland, the name given by Jansz and
other Dutch explorers to the land when they first found
and rejected it.

Cook set out again in 1772. After crisscrossing the
vast Pacific as far as Antarctica, he proved once and for
all that most of the ocean was empty. If there were a
great southern land anywhere, it must have been the land
he had seen.

A Prison Colony

Shortly, England would have great use for the land
Cook had claimed. England was experiencing terrible
social problems. Its cities, London being the worst case,
were overrun by unemployed people. Slums grew and
spread. Widespread crime added more trouble. To pre-

serve order, the government enacted harsh laws under which people could be given long prison sentences for very minor crimes, even for being unable to pay debts. So many people were imprisoned that the jails overflowed and people feared the spread of disease. Rotting ships that were tied up along the Thames River in London were turned into jails. They were crammed full of men, women, and children who had run afoul of the law. Conditions were horrible and all Londoners were appalled and frightened.

The solution was to send prisoners to the far colonies. There, they could work off their sentences as laborers in the new settlements, under the control of colonial governors and troops. This practice was known as "transportation." A criminal or a debtor was not sentenced to prison but was given transportation to one of the colonies. Under the terms of transportation, convicts could earn their freedom eventually, when they had worked off enough years to pay for the crime.

Authorities sent some convicts to America. But, by 1770 when Captain Cook sailed into Botany Bay, the American colonies were already displaying the restlessness and itch for freedom that would result in the United States' Declaration of Independence. No longer able to use America as a prison, or penal, colony, England's eye fell upon Australia. In May 1787, eleven ships under the command of Captain Arthur Phillip sailed from London for Australia carrying about 1,000 passengers, three-fourths of them convicts.

Landing in Sydney

It took Captain Phillip's little fleet eight months to reach Botany Bay. He anchored there briefly and sent scouts up and down the coast. They reported a much more desirable and safer harbor just to the north, and so Phillip sailed there. This place is called Port Jackson or Sydney Harbor, and it was there, on January 26, 1788, that Phillip sent the first white Australians ashore.

Phillip's brave ships are known to Australians as the First Fleet. His landing at Sydney Harbor is celebrated every year as part of Australia Day ceremonies. Phillip named Sydney for Viscount Sydney, the secretary of the department of the English government that supervised colonial affairs. It was the first settlement in Australia. Sydney has always been the seat of government for New South Wales, Australia's first and most populous state.

The Aborigines

The Aborigines watched from the shore as Captain Phillip landed the first white settlers. No one asked the Aborigines' permission to come ashore; no one ever negotiated with them for land. They did not resist the

The early settlers hoisted the British flag when the First Fleet landed at Sydney Harbor.

landing. What they did, by all accounts, was watch the whites unload their ships and come ashore.

To the white settlers, the Aborigines were primitive savages. They had built no towns or cities. They knew nothing of Western civilization or its rules and manners. Many went about naked.

The few settlers who did take an interest in the Aborigines usually tried to convert them, clothe them, and teach them white ways. Some whites treated them as curiosities. Many more whites showed the Aborigines terrible cruelty. Aborigines were killed because they were regarded as thieves, and sometimes just because they were regarded as a nuisance. The Aborigines did little to help their own cause. When they learned the whites had stores of food, some Aborigines stopped hunting and fishing, and begged because begging was easier work. Although some Aborigines fought the whites, they never teamed up to make an effective fighting force.

Whites took the best land. Because the Aborigines never built anything on the land, whites assumed it was available to them. Although whites employed some Aborigines as herders and trackers in the Outback, whites were always boss. The Aborigines were driven to the outskirts of Australian society.

The Early Pioneers

The early days of Australia's first settlement were very grim. The wheat seed that the settlers had brought from England spoiled during the journey and would not germinate when planted in Australia. Their sheep were taken by Aborigines or stolen by convicts up to their old tricks. There was nothing to buy in Australia and the settlers were unable to grow anything. Before long, the new colony, existing on ships' supplies, was on half-rations and in real trouble.

About thirty months after the first settlers landed, a new ship appeared in the harbor. Those on shore hoped it carried a new supply of food. Instead, it carried more convicts, many of them aged and ill, and they only added to the misery of the colony. But fortunately, the Second Fleet, carrying food, new seed, more animals, and healthy reinforcements of people, followed not far behind and the colony was saved.

A total of about 160,000 convicts from England, including many rebellious Irish, were sent to Australia before transportation officially ended in 1868. Very few of the convicts were women, so from the beginning Australia was a heavily male society.

In the earliest decades, naval officers had full authority to govern the settlement of Sydney. Some were cruel to the convicts under their control, and to the Aborigines. Many were more interested in their own welfare than the colony's, and they shaped laws to make profits for themselves.

The convicts, hard to control, found it easy to flee the corrupt administration of the Sydney colony. Many of them went into the countryside, found land they could live on, and took possession of it as squatters. Some of them, too, built ranches and farms from which they made good livings and sometimes fortunes.

Between the convicts and the greedy administrators, there was as much disorder as order in the early years of colonization. To that can be added the dangers and disappointments that could be expected in a new and strange land.

Making Order Out of Chaos

The first sense of real order came in 1810. Lachlan Macquarie was appointed governor of the colony of New South Wales with Sydney as its headquarters. Macquarie broke the monopolies of the naval adminis-trators or "rum corps," established the first Australian currency and the first bank, and encouraged public works and town planning. Also at this time, free settlers who were not criminals were encouraged to come to Australia.

Meanwhile, the first Australians were beginning to learn a few things about their adopted home. George Bass, a naval surgeon, and Matthew Flinders, a naval officer, sailed out in 1795 to explore the great coastlines. In 1798 they sailed around Tasmania, proving it was an island. In 1801 Flinders was given permission to mount an expedition to chart the entire coast of Australia. He sailed for three years and when he was finished, England and the colonists knew for certain that Australia was an island, with water on all sides.

Finally, the world knew that this was indeed the long-hidden great southern land. Adapting the old name

Terra Australis Incognita, it was finally and officially given the name Australia.

Exploring Unknown Land

Meanwhile, the settlers were also curious about the interior of Australia. Macquarie, in addition to everything else he did for the new colony, encouraged exploration inland. Before his term in office ended in 1821, a milestone was passed. The crossing of the Blue Mountains, a difficult natural barrier about 100 miles (about 160 kilometers) inland from Sydney, took place in 1813. Farmers and ranchers had spread out north and south of Sydney. Parramatta, at the western end of Sydney Harbor, was a wonderfully fertile farming area. But the mountains had kept settlement hemmed in until this time.

Other early explorers followed the major rivers of New South Wales. In 1830 Charles Sturt set out with a party on the Murrumbidgee River. He then followed the Lachlan and the Murray rivers. Because rivers flowed west, it was assumed that they emptied into a great inland sea. This would promise a fertile middle country. Sturt got as far as Lake Alexandria, near present-day Adelaide, but he found no inland sea. His party was forced back the way they had come, against the rivers' currents. Sturt was left temporarily blind by the experience. Other explorers clung to the idea that there had to be an inland sea in the interior, but like Sturt they found only disappointment or death.

While Sturt and others suffered heroically, expansion was taking place along the coasts, which were reachable by sailing vessels. Port Phillip, where Melbourne would be built beginning in 1835, was first settled in 1803. A settlement was started on Tasmania the following year. In 1825 the Bathurst and Melville islands off the north coast were claimed as English property. In 1827 a permanent and lonely settlement was begun on the coast of the Indian Ocean at Albany, the first settlement of Western Australia.

Adelaide's first settlers arrived in 1835, the same year as Melbourne's. In 1829, Captain James Stirling (who had already had a look at the Swan River, which empties into the Indian Ocean on the west coast) led the settlers who would build the city of Perth.

Resourceful Colonists

In the early years each of these colonies lived on steadfastness, resourcefulness, and little else. Australians were still trying to adjust to a new climate and harsh new surroundings. Occasionally they had trouble with Aborigines. Sometimes disease spread quickly.

But everywhere the explorers went, people followed, driven by the instinct to be free, and the prospect of owning their own land. The rule was that people could have whatever land they claimed. These settlers were called squatters. There was no previous owner to be paid and Australia provided more than enough land for everyone. The squatters weren't at all sure what could be raised on their land, but at least it was theirs.

It was John MacArthur, once a Sydney administrator, who found a use for the vast interior and who fueled the squatters' rush for land. MacArthur had been a farmer as well as a naval officer. He thought the climate and foliage of the scrubland between the sea and the interior deserts resembled Spain, where sheep thrived and supported a wool industry. MacArthur imported merino sheep from Spain and they proved him right. Not only could these animals tolerate the heat of the interior, but they could survive in areas where the grass was thin and the soil too rocky for farming. MacArthur's merinos were of supreme importance. They gave Australia its first economy, and also the first indication that the hardship of settlement might be worth something.

Oddly enough, the camel was important to Australia's history as well. Camels, not native to Australia, were imported from Afghanistan. For years before there were real roads, they carried supplies to the settlements deep in the Red Center. Horses had quickly failed the early explorers, so they turned to camels, which were used to living in arid deserts.

Today, farming is very important to Australia's economy. Crops grow in the green and hilly farmland near Melbourne.

Eventually Australians developed a cattle industry. There was some whaling along the coasts. Wheat farming was tried and it, too, expanded until it became an important industry.

While Australians learned what to do with the land under their feet, their explorers like Edward John Eyre and Robert O'Hara Burke pressed farther and farther inland for a look at the land still unmapped. The idea of a fertile middle area still attracted them. Some journeyed

Setting up camps to pan gold, people flocked to Australia in search of riches in the days of the Gold Rush.

out and never returned. The explorers who survived won lasting fame. But the answer they brought back was the same that Sturt had returned with. There was no inland sea watering a fertile center. The center was a terrible desert, unbelievably hostile to humans.

Then this harsh land popped its surprise. As worthless as much of it appeared on the surface, it was rich underneath. Gold was discovered in 1851 in Bathurst, west of Sydney, and it brought profound change with it.

Sailors and clerks left their posts in the cities and the ports and headed for Bathurst. Melbourne is said to have almost emptied of men during the gold rush. By July of 1851, rich gold mines were in operation in towns such as Bendigo and Ballarat, and a boom was on. Word spread beyond Australia, and thousands and thousands of new immigrants flocked Down Under to get in on the riches.

4. Independence at Last

In 1868 the transportation of convicts from England stopped and Australia began to take stock of itself. There were six separate colonies: New South Wales, Victoria, South Australia, Queensland, Western Australia, and Tasmania. Each was separately chartered by Great Britain, and not much cooperation existed between the colonies. The British government appointed governors for the colonies and closely supervised the laws and development of each. Beginning about 1875 Britain started to extend a little freedom to the colonies by giving them self-governing status. After this, the colonies could organize their own elections and write laws for themselves, but always under the watchful eye of London.

Finally, Queen Victoria announced that Australia would receive status as a nation on January 1, 1901. The new country would be a full-fledged commonwealth within the British Empire, made up of all its six colonies.

Australia's first constitution was fairly limited. Great Britain would continue to handle Australia's foreign affairs. Laws passed in London would take priority over Australia's own laws; if there was a conflict, London law ruled. Australia could set up its own courts, but anyone who didn't like the ruling of an Australian judge could appeal the decision to a British one. Independence was a big step, but like a toddler, Australia did not stray far from Mother England's skirts. For years after achieving its independence, the country's national anthem remained, "God Save the Queen." At last, many years later, the country chose its own anthem, "Advance Australia Fair."

World War I

Great Britain expected Australia's help in its wars, and Australia did not fail it. Aussies fought in the Boer Wars in South Africa on Great Britain's side and, a decade later in 1914 they joined the British and other Allies in fighting World War I.

World War I gave birth to the ANZACs, as the soldiers of the Australian and New Zealand Army Corps were called. The two countries combined their forces. The first group of them stopped in Egypt on their way to the trenches of France and Belgium. Along with the British, French, and other colonial troops, they were assembled into a force that was ordered to land on the Gallipoli Peninsula and drive the Turkish enemy toward the Black Sea. The invasion was poorly planned and the Allied Force was pinned down on the beaches for weeks. Thirty-five thousand Allies died, and 3,500 of them were

In Palestine, Aussie troops line up from the Ninth Australian Division in World War I.

ANZACs. But many were still to die in the trenches of Europe. In all, the Australians killed in World War I totaled about 60,000, a shocking number for a new nation.

World War II

After the war, in the 1930s, the world economy slumped, and so did Australia's. Nearly one third of the work force was unemployed, and many companies went

People crowd in front of the capitol building in Canberra on ANZAC Day to remember the soldiers killed in war.

bankrupt. Great Britain declared war on Germany again in 1939, at the outset of World War II. And again, Australia answered the call of the Empire. ANZACs fought in North Africa and in the Mediterranean. But World War II was different, because this time Australia itself was in danger. The Japanese entered the war in 1941 with their attack on Pearl Harbor. They soon over-ran much of Asia and the Pacific, and Australia had to think of itself. When Japanese aircraft bombed Australia's Darwin in 1942, the threat of invasion seemed real. England, under attack at home, could not help Australia, but America could.

A wartime partnership and a lasting friendship sprang up between the Aussies and the Yanks, who fought alongside each other at the important Battle of the Coral Sea, and when the Japanese were rolled back almost island by island in the Pacific.

At home, Australia flourished after World War II. There was an explosion of growth around the world. Most nations, having weathered the Great Depression of the 1930s only to be thrown into war, at last celebrated peace. Those countries which suffered the most during the war were rebuilt. All were hungry customers for the raw materials and agricultural products that Australia supplied in abundance.

After World War II, Australia, New Zealand, and the United States signed a mutual defense agreement called the ANZUS Treaty. In it, each agreed to help the other if any were attacked in the Pacific. Australia, like most other countries in the world, became a member of the United Nations, which held out the hope that there might never be more attacks anywhere. But there were more wars, although they were smaller. Australian troops lined up with the Americans again during the Korean and Vietnam wars.

With World War II, the world entered the nuclear

age. The strain of the invention of terrible weapons
eventually ended the ANZUS partnership. New Zealand
was ushered out in 1986. Its government refused to allow
U.S. Navy ships armed with nuclear weapons or pow-
ered by nuclear engines to call at its ports any longer.
Those who wish to freeze the production of nuclear
weapons have urged the Australian government to enact
the same ban, thus far without success. But Australia has
strictly limited the mining of uranium and it agreed in
1985 to designate the entire South Pacific region a
nuclear-free zone. Whether Australia and the United
States remain close friends and allies probably depends
somewhat on the course of nuclear politics.

The Immigrants Pour In

Australia needed to increase its population after the
war to regain strength as a nation. Hoping to do just
that, Australia opened its doors to European immigrants
in the 1940s. The government began a special program to
encourage homeless European war victims to find shelter in Australia. So many moved to Australia, that by the
the time the 1940s ended, Australia was beginning to
come out of its geographic isolation.

Before, Australia was mostly a British country with
British people. The flood of Italians, Greeks, Germans,
Dutch, and Yugoslavs changed the entire social structure

of Australia. More than two million people came between 1945 and 1965. They were responsible for much of the work force in the 1950s and 1960s—developing factories, mines, roads, and steelworks. Today, one quarter of Australia's population is immigrants and their children.

Up until the 1970s, Australia had a "whites only" immigration policy that excluded all Asians from entering the country. Since then, many have come to Australia from China and Southeast Asia. Now, about one third of Australian immigrants are Asian. Australia has always had trade relations with this part of the world, and the South Pacific region is becoming increasingly important in world trade.

Australia's Changing Economy

In the past years, Australia has undergone a major trade shift. Before, Australia's main economy was based on sheep, wheat, and other agricultural products. Government officials have worried that Australia's raw materials will become less important to customer nations that seem to be turning more to technology for strength. Now, Australia's most valuable resources are uranium and other manufactured products.

In the past, Great Britain has been Australia's biggest trade customer. Since the 1960s Australia has spread its trade to other countries. Japan is now Australia's chief trade partner. It buys coal, iron ore, minerals, wheat, and wool. The United States is the second biggest customer, buying beef, sugar, and bauxite. Australia's neighbor country, New Zealand, also trades with Australia.

By world standards, Australians have a high standard of living and great freedom of lifestyles. Unfortunately, the lucky land is not without its problems. Unemployment is higher than ever, and the gap between rich and poor is often great.

The government is struggling to combat the slipping economy, and to maintain the sense of freedom and prosperity that Australians have come to enjoy. The tourist industry is booming as more and more people learn about Australia from movies about the bush life and the sparkling seashores. But Australia is more than a land of swagmen and kangaroos!

5. The Natural Australia

Australia has many distinctive animals. Some, like the koala and the kangaroo, are found nowhere else in the world. Most experts believe this is due to Australia's isolation. Because the continent is surrounded by the sea on all sides, Australia's animal species evolved there and there alone, and could not travel to other lands. Most of Australia's animals are not valuable sources of either food or labor, so they were not transported to other countries when white settlers landed.

No one is sure where the kangaroo came from, and no one is sure if kangaroos ever lived anywhere besides in Australia and on a few surrounding islands. Kangaroos are marsupials, a word describing mammals that give birth to under-developed young. Because they need time to grow, the babies must be carried in the mother's pouch for a while after they are born. The kangaroos' young, for as long as they ride about in the pouch, are called "joeys." Different types of marsupials exist in North and South America and in Asia. But experts say that in those places, they did not have the time to develop as they did in Australia. This continent lay largely un-populated for many centuries and was introduced to white civilization later than other areas. Australia has

125 separate species of marsupials, ranging from tiny mice to the big red kangaroo, which stands more than six feet tall.

The Kangaroo

Of all the marsupials, the kangaroo is the best known. It has become practically a symbol of Australia. A kangaroo wearing boxing gloves appeared on the sails of Australia's challenge boat in the 1983 America's Cup. When the boat won, this "boxing kangaroo" appeared on tea towels, coffee mugs, T-shirts, tote bags, swimsuits, and license plates.

More than forty separate varieties of kangaroo live in Australia including the brawny big red, the half-sized wallaby, and even smaller breeds. They all run with the same distinctive hop. They are much faster than it appears they would be, and city-dwelling Australians and and travelers get very excited when they see them. When a herd of kangaroos, all in a line, hop a fence to cross a country road, the sight resembles a ballet performed by gifted acrobats.

Yet kangaroos are a terrible nuisance. They dash into the roads without looking, making them a serious hazard to drivers. Practically everyone who lives in the rural districts has hit a kangaroo while driving at night. Most of the people in small towns put special iron bars over the

A kangaroo sits with its baby "joey" poking its head out of its mother's pouch. Both are chewing on yellow flowers called "wattle."

fronts of their cars and trucks to protect against collisions with kangaroos. Some install heavy screens over the windshields, since many kangaroos are big enough to badly damage a vehicle and injure its occupants.

Kangaroos are herbivores, which means they eat grass, seeds, and leaves. In dry weather, they gather near the roads to eat in the grassy ditches. It is not unusual to find the roadside littered with dead kangaroos in the morning during these periods, all of them killed by cars and trucks.

To farmers and ranchers, the kangaroo is a serious pest. It eats grass meant for the sheep, and eats and tramples crops. Big ones break down fences, letting a farmer's sheep roam into other pastures. Each year, by permission of the government, hunters shoot thousands and thousands of kangaroos, just to keep a balance between them and the sheep and cattle. Sometimes farmers and ranchers don't think the official kangaroo kill goes far enough, so they go out on their own unauthorized hunts and kill more. Animal lovers complain about this, but the kangaroo population is so large that most varieties are not really in any danger of extinction.

Other Aussie Mammals

The koala, which also nurses its young in a pouch after birth, is as cuddly as it looks, and is gentle, too. It

A sleepy koala gets all the attention in a Koala Park outside of Sydney.

has long claws because it lives in trees and must be able to climb, but it pulls in its claws when you handle it. The koala is a fussy animal. It lives in the branches of the eucalyptus tree, eating leaves from which it gets both food and water. The koala's Aboriginal name means "one who doesn't drink." Australia has five to six hundred different varieties of eucalyptus, and the koala will only eat the leaves of the kind of tree in which it was born. If a koala finds itself in the wrong kind of eucalyptus tree, it will starve rather than try a new diet. Because the koala has poor eyesight, in daylight as well as in darkness, it has a hard time finding its way home if it is lost. Koalas stay in their trees almost all of the time. If they come down, it is at night, and then they do not wander.

When early Australians discovered the koala and learned how soft its fur was, they hunted it so vigorously that there was fear for its survival. Finally, the government passed strict laws prohibiting koala hunting and protecting its habitat. Koalas still live in the forests of eastern Australia, free and wild. They are not easy to find, since they hide in their trees. But in the special koala parks near most of the big cities, you can watch them climb, eat, and sleep. You can even pet them!

The wombat is another Australian marsupial. It is a husky, longhaired animal built close to the ground like a pig. It burrows underground, and it eats roots and

The duck-billed, egg-laying platypus is one of Australia's strangest native animals.

leaves. Although the wombat is not cute like the koala or acrobatic like the kangaroo, it deserves mention because it is another animal found only in Australia.

Monotremes are primitive mammals that lay eggs. Australia has two monotremes, the echidna or spiny anteater, and the platypus. The echidna, with its coarse brown hair and sharp spines, looks something like a hedgehog. It lives on termites and ants. The platypus has a thick coat of brown fur, webbed feet, and a ducklike bill. It lives along western Australia's streams, rivers, and lakes. This unusual animal uses its long bill to scoop up worms, small shellfish, and other animals as it swims along. As endangered species, both the echidna and the platypus are protected and cannot be hunted or captured without the government's authorization.

The dingo is Australia's famous wild dog. It is believed that the dingo was brought to the continent by the Aborigines when they themselves migrated from Southeast Asia. Dingoes are Australia's chief beasts of prey and among the country's few meat-eating animals. They will attack sheep, cattle, and kangaroos. Dingoes are rust-colored and mean-looking and their wailing howls can be frightening.

Reptiles

Australia is full of reptiles, including 140 species of snakes and 370 species of lizards. Reptiles, particularly the great monitor and goanna lizards, figure importantly in Aboriginal culture. Along a highway south of Darwin is a low, tilted rock formation that resembles the monitor lizard. Tribes of the area believe that the spirit that created the earth adopted the shape of the monitor after its work was done, and now lives in that rock. The rock is a protected, sacred site. Goannas six feet in length have been captured alive. The lizard that appears on more

A crocodile swims along the Adelaide River in the Northern Territory.

postcards than any other is the unusual frill-necked lizard of the desert. When it scents danger, flaps alongside its head extend and it looks as if the lizard is wearing a high ruffled collar.

Crocodiles live in the bays and coastal rivers of the Northern Territory and Queensland. The crocodiles are very dangerous reptiles, and every year human lives are lost to them. They will bump people out of canoes and flatboats and will snatch them off the banks.

Australia's Native Birds

Many visitors to Australia are surprised at its immense variety of bird life. In fact, Australia has around seven hundred species of native birds. The countryside is full of eagles, hawks, geese, egrets, cockatoos, and many others, including parrots. They range in size from an emu, which resembles the ostrich and towers over the tallest kangaroo, to the tiny lily walker, smaller than a child's fist.

Emu stroll around the countryside, usually in pairs, troubling neither man nor beast. They are fun to watch. They look silly, with their very thin legs, fat bodies, and long thin necks, but they are very dignified-looking at the same time. Emu are also very social creatures. If you wave to them from your car, they will walk over and peer in to see if they know you. Emu eggs, bigger than grapefruits, were prized by Aborigines, who would cook the insides after carefully removing them from the shells. The eggshells, preserved whole, are almost leathery. Today, Aborigines carve designs and pictures on the shells, and these are sold in souvenir shops.

The lily walker is found along the ponds and streams of the Northern Territory. The female lays her eggs on a lily pad, and it is the male's job to protect them. When something makes waves that rock the lily pad—perhaps a goose landing or a crocodile entering the water—the

Emus, as big as ostriches, strut through the countryside.

male races furiously around the edges of the lily pad, keeping it level and preventing the eggs from rolling into the water.

Other birds are unique to Australia as well. One is the kookaburra. Known for its noisy cackle, it is generally called the "laughing kookaburra." Australia's entry in the 1987 America's Cup race at Perth was named the *Kookaburra* after this bird. The galah, pronounced gah-LAH, is a white bird about the size of a pigeon. Galahs are everywhere in the Outback, always traveling in great flocks. When something spooks them and the whole group rises from the earth, you can see that each of them has bright pink feathers under its wings. When they fly off, the galahs seem to streak the sky with pink.

Australia even has penguins—a variety known as fairy penguins. They live on the beaches of Phillip Island off Melbourne. At dusk, they come ashore and return to the sandy burrows where they live. Many Australians, and tourists as well, go to Phillip Island just to see the little penguins come home every evening.

Australian Flora

The variety of trees, plants, and flowers is almost endless in Australia. Eucalyptus trees thrive in practically every soil and climate of the country. They are also known as gum trees, and varieties range from bushes shorter than the average human to towering giants. Many of the gums are recognizable by their swollen trunks and gnarled, twisted limbs. Acacia trees, particularly the variety known as the mulga, are also found all over Australia. In northern Queensland, there are rain forests where trees are jungle-thick and hung with vines and creepers. In the deserts, trees are few and far between. The few that are there look dwarfed and barely nourished, as if they are struggling to survive.

Gum trees such as this one are found throughout Australia. The old local name for this tree is the Blue Gum, but it is also known as the Forest Red Gum.

One tree found in Australia, the southern beech, is also found in South America and South Africa. The reason that the same tree is found in three different parts of the world is that scientists believe that much of the Southern Hemisphere was once all one land mass, not separated by oceans as its parts are today.

Wildflowers grow all over Australia, and in the scrubland and the deserts, they put on an extraordinary show. These empty deserts are dull and colorless in the dry seasons, as if all life were parched out of them. Trees and grass dry up and begin to turn brown. With a downpour, the picture changes dramatically. Green reappears as if by magic and all over the landscape, wildflowers bloom in great numbers. Red and pink, blue and white, orange and yellow, they blanket the countryside. It is a glorious sight.

6. *Australia Celebrates*

Australians love to celebrate, and their calendars are full of holidays, festivals, and commemorations. Some, such as Christmas, New Year's Day, and Easter, are celebrated much as Americans celebrate them. Some are English holidays and are celebrated in all the countries that once made up the British Empire. Some are purely Australian.

For Aussies Only

The two main Australia-only holidays have fixed dates and everyone celebrates them at the same time. One is joyous, and the other is solemn. Australia Day, the happy occasion, is celebrated on January 26. It commemorates the arrival of the first white settlers aboard the First Fleet of Captain Phillip in 1788. This was modern Australia's beginning, and like the United States' Independence Day on July 4, this holiday evokes memories of everything Australian.

On Australia Day, the landing at Sydney Harbor is reenacted. Children dress up in historical costumes and play famous people from the past in pageants throughout the country. Special concerts celebrate Australian

This is a 1983 re-enactment of Australia Day in Sydney Harbor. The ship resembles the First Fleet, as it sails in front of the famous Sydney Opera House.

talent and sporting contests and tournaments add to the festivity.

One of the biggest Australia Day celebrations ever will take place in 1988, because that is the two hundredth anniversary of the arrival of the first white settlers. The highlight of the celebrations in 1988 will be the dedication of the new national capitol buildings in Canberra.

The solemn commemoration is ANZAC Day, which occurs on April 25 of every year. It honors the many men who fought and died overseas for Australia and for England. Surviving veterans parade in their old uniforms, and the former commanders make speeches. Trumpeters play sad salutes to the fallen. The Boer War is remembered, as are the Gallipoli invasion, and the trenches of France and Belgium. From the days of World War II, men talk about the Desert Campaign in Africa and the terrible fighting against the Japanese on the Kokoda Trail in New Guinea. Younger men recall the Korean War and Vietnam. ANZAC Day is a reminder that progress often demands sacrifice. Every year speakers express the wish that the world will one day learn to progress without more wars.

Other National Holidays

Another major holiday remembers the British Empire and Australia's part in it. This is Commonwealth Day, celebrated in May every year. When the British Empire was dissolved after World War II, roughly over the years from 1948 to 1965, it was replaced by the British Commonwealth. The nations that made up the Empire were, one by one, granted total self-rule and independence. But they all had common ties to England, and continued to meet as equals to discuss world affairs among themselves.

Although no single country can tell the others what

to do, they felt they could perhaps be a force for good and for peace in the world. Queen Elizabeth II of England is a great supporter of the Commonwealth, and takes her honorary position as head of it very seriously. The forty-nine nations of the Commonwealth meet in a different country every year, most of them represented by their highest officials.

Labor Day, although it is much the same the world over, has special meaning in Australia, where the man who digs a ditch is as proud of what he does as the businessman who makes million-dollar deals. Every working man and woman celebrates Labor Day in Australia. Just as in America, it is a day of speeches, politics, and picnics. Labor Day is celebrated on many different dates in Australia—depending on the area.

Sometimes sporting events are occasions for public holidays in Australia. Adelaide Cup Day is a holiday that celebrates a big horse race. Melbourne Cup Day is a public holiday so that everyone can spend the day watching the race. Once a year, the small Outback town of Alice Springs hosts a camel race, and tourists can see many camels in the nearby camel farms.

Australia's Cultural Blend

The many immigrants from other lands and other cultures have enriched the Australian calendar with new

The finish of the 1986 Melbourne Cup horse races is an exciting moment for all the spectators.

holidays and festivals. Chinese New Year's, although not a day off from work or school, is celebrated wherever the Chinese find themselves. It is a festival of food and entertainment. Historically, it is also a time when the Chinese settle any debts they have and start anew.

Hungarians commemorate their unsuccessful 1956 uprising against their Communist government every October. In Australia as well as in America, it is a sad day of remembrance. Other peoples, such as the Greeks

Playing the didgeridoo and dancing, these Aborigines partici-pate in their traditional festival, the corroboree.

and the Italians, have their own celebrations as well. Some are religious, centering around the churches. All add to the flavor of the new and worldly Australia.

The famous traditional festivals of the Aborigines are called corroboree (kah-ROB-oh-ree). Corroboree might be held in celebration, perhaps for deliverance from a drought or other danger. It might be a religious festival, held in honor of the guarding spirits. Often it marks the initiation of young boys into full manhood.

Aborigine men take the main roles at corroboree. They paint their bodies, and they dance. They are skilled at mimicking the movements of the animals. Corroboree might include sporting contests, such as who can throw a spear the farthest and straightest, and who can make a boomerang do the most tricks. Music at corroboree usually comes from a didgeridoo, a long hollow tube played by mouth that makes a mournful sound.

Women usually have a secondary role at corroboree. They prepare the feast, and they might attend as part of the audience, but the performances are left to the men. When corroboree involves initiation, only men and boys attend. Women hold their own initiation ceremonies for young girls, and men are forbidden to attend these.

Corroboree is almost always a private celebration, open only to members of a particular tribe of Aborigines. However, Aborigines perform their traditional dances and play the didgeridoo for tourists at various Outback hotels and other locations, so everyone can get a glimpse of the ceremony.

Christian Holidays and New Year's Day

Christmas is celebrated on December 25, as it is everywhere, and is the time when people celebrate the birth of Christ. It is also a chance for families to unite, and is a time of major gift-giving to family, friends, and loved ones. People take short holidays then, and children are out of school.

But there is one big difference in the Australian Christmas. December 25 in Australia falls in summer because their seasons are opposite of America's. Many Australians make it a tradition to go to the beach on Christmas, while many Americans go outdoors in the snow. Family Christmas pictures in Australia often show a Christmas tree stuck in the sand and the family grouped around it. Father Christmas comes to the beach (sometimes in shorts), and the gifts he leaves are wrapped in paper that shows reindeer in the snow. Everything about an Australian Christmas would be familiar to Americans except for the summer weather.

The day after Christmas in Australia and all the Commonwealth countries is called Boxing Day. Boxing Day, traditionally, is the day when people used to put their leftovers from Christmas in boxes for the poor. Now, people leave small gifts or tips for the postman, the newsboy, the grocer, and the butcher. These are little gifts to say thank you for good service.

Boxing Day in an old English custom. The coming of labor unions, which guarantees a minimum wage for most working people, has removed some of the original reasons for Boxing Day. Even errand boys no longer have to depend on tips. However, no one likes to let go of a holiday once it is established, and Boxing Day con-

Fireworks light up Sydney Harbor on New Year's Eve.

tinues. Since most people are off work on Boxing Day, the stores are usually full, and the day marks the beginning of the big after-Christmas sales.

Easter, as in the rest of the world, usually takes place on a different Sunday each year, depending on the church calendar. As in America, Easter is an important religious occasion, marking the Resurrection of Christ. Of course, Good Friday and Easter come in the autumn in Australia. Children sometimes dye Easter eggs like American children do, but it is much more common for them to hunt for chocolate eggs, or Easter baskets.

New Year's Day is January 1 and is another "summer" holiday in Australia. As everywhere else, it is a time to remember the year just past and to start a new one. Australians are optimistic people, and the beginning of a new year is something they celebrate with great enthusiasm.

7. All the Comforts of Home

Three out of four Australians live in cities, most of them in the green and sunny belt of coastline that runs from Brisbane on the eastern coast to Adelaide on the southern coast. Despite all the attention the Outback gets, Australia is one of the most urbanized countries in the world. The typical Australian city layout—a tiny central city surrounded by a number of residential or suburban areas—is found throughout the British Commonwealth countries. All of them copied London, England, the principal city of the old British Empire. London has a small "city" area with Greater London spread about it. All the big Australian cities—Sydney, Brisbane, Melbourne, Adelaide, Perth, and Darwin—are laid out on this plan. The design is even the same in smaller cities like Alice Springs, which is the main city of the Outback but has fewer than 30,000 residents.

The Suburban Sydney

Sydney, the country's largest city, is a good example of a sprawling, heavily populated coastal area. Its downtown, (the actual "city of Sydney") is quite small in area, occupying only about 15 square miles (about 24 square

Sparkling Sydney (next two pages) is a coastal city that stretches inland and is surrounded by suburbs.

kilometers). Here, skyscrapers stand on the slope of land rising from the harbor where the first settlers landed. All around this small downtown area spread the suburbs and far suburbs that make up greater Sydney. Sydney reaches more than 100 miles (160 kilometers) north and south along the Pacific coast. It stretches more than 50 miles (80 kilometers) west to the Blue Mountains.

This sprawling city includes thirty-one separate municipalities and many, many more residential communities. It covers over 3,000 square miles (4,800 square kilometers) and it offers residents of Sydney many choices of living styles.

Many residents of Sydney live on the water. Not only is there the Pacific coastline, but Sydney Harbor itself extends inland for miles. Waterfront homes are prized, and this is where some of Sydney's most expensive areas are found.

Outside of downtown Sydney, the suburbs cluster together, one after the other, across land that is sometimes flat, sometimes rolling. There are communities of every character. Some are built around modern shopping centers; others resemble old-fashioned villages. In some, the houses sit close together on city-sized lots, and in others the houses are more spread out. The coastal belt of greater Sydney gets enough rain to keep it green much of the year, and the farthest suburbs have a nice country look.

Most of the communities that make up greater Sydney are complete "mini-cities" in themselves. They have their own schools, churches, and recreational facilities, and include community business districts and shopping centers.

A modern and very efficient system of commuter trains links Sydney with its far-flung suburbs, and this is how most working people get to downtown jobs. There are no auto expressways, as we know them. Still, owning a car is very important to the average Australian, and cars are necessary for getting from one suburb to another.

City Housing

Australians believe strongly in a separate house for each family, so there are very few apartment buildings. It is estimated that 75 percent of Australians are buying their own homes. Most of the newer Australian homes are one-story buildings made of wood and brick, or wood and stone. Americans would call them ranch homes. Australia is a country of low buildings; in fact it did not have skyscrapers until the 1950s. Most suburban homes are surrounded by lawns and have attached garages.

An earlier type of Australian home is found in the close-in residential areas of cities like Sydney. These are

These houses cover the hills of Melbourne, and are typical of Australian architecture.

all-wood homes and they have two distinct features—they have low porches one step up from the ground across the entire front of them, and they are decorated with trellis-like trim. Since housing lots are smaller in the older parts of the cities, these homes are usually close together with only a narrow walkway separating one from another.

New or old, Australian homes have one thing in common: the most important room in the house is the living room. Australians call it the "lounge." A typical Australian lounge will include a comfortable couch or two, several chairs, a large table, a television, a bookcase, and often a mantel displaying the family photographs.

The lounge is where everyone gathers at the end of the day. Children do their homework at the table and the couch is always placed for the best television viewing. The family always entertains visitors in the lounge, and sometimes eats meals there. A house without a good-sized lounge wouldn't seem a house at all to many Australians.

Entertainment in the City

In Sydney, families enjoy entertainment that ranges from the Opera House to the cabaret theaters where Australia's sassy humor is exhibited, to rock and roll clubs. Its many movie theaters present the best films from around the world, as well as the many fine films made in Australia. The main libraries and museums are near the city center. The Rocks, the actual point where the first settlers landed, has been transformed from an aging, dirty warehouse district into a showplace of shops and restaurants. At Circular Quay, Sydney residents board ferryboats that carry them across the harbor to the Sydney Zoo, or up and down the harbor on excursion rides. There are many fine restaurants, so many that

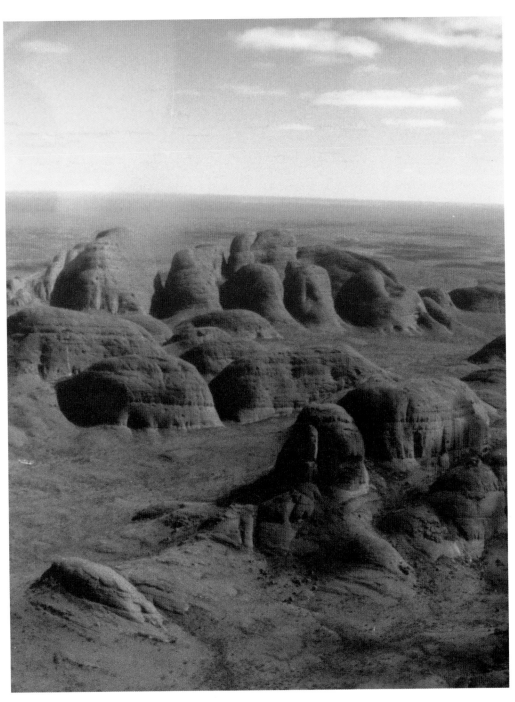

The Outback is full of interesting rock formations. These mystical rocks, called Olgas, are known as "Heads" to the Aborigines.

people say you can find any cuisine of the world in Sydney.

Australia's other cities offer similar types of amusement and entertainment. Each of Australia's state capitals has a permanent company of professional actors and actresses that performs classical and modern plays year-round, as well as a professional symphony orchestra. The Australian Opera and the Australian Ballet also keep the Aussies entertained.

Outback Living

Life in the Outback is much different from city life. Immense distances separate places in the Great Empty. Cities are few and far between, and the towns are very small. Sheep ranches and farms can be many thousands of acres in size, and the people who live on them may get to town only once a week, and to major cities no more than once or twice a year.

Farm and ranch homes in the Outback tend to be large, sprawling places because they have to serve many purposes. One part of the house contains the office of the farm or ranch. Homes have to be big enough to accommodate overnight company since almost every visitor stays the night. Each house has large storerooms and pantries, because farm families have to stock up heavily on food and supplies when they shop in town. Most farms and ranches have a family garden where they grow some of their food.

Since towns are so far away, farm and ranch families must provide their own entertainment. Many homes have swimming pools. Indoors, there might be billiard tables and ping-pong tables. People living in the Outback have television, just like city residents do, though they don't receive as many channels. Video cassette recorders, or VCRs, are popular. When nothing is on television, Outback families will show home movies, or videotapes of family weddings and other occasions.

The vast countryside itself provides many opportunities for recreation. Families hunt and even fish if they are near a river that flows year-round. They ride horses and sometimes take motorbikes on trail rides. When many friends and relatives gather for a big picnic, ranch hands will often go out and corral two kangaroos of equal size. Then the highlight of the picnic will be kangaroo races.

When ranch families go to town, a lot of the trip's enjoyment comes from just visiting with town friends and catching up on the news. Most small towns have a movie theater. Almost every town has a chapter of the Returned Servicemen's League, an organization much like the American Legion. Often its clubhouse is the center of social activity for the area.

Australians living on ranches and farms in the Outback rely heavily on each other. Homesteads are linked

An Outback child and her lamb. There are more sheep than people in Australia!

by two-way radio. Families share vital information such as the condition of roads and wildfire warnings, and they pass on emergency calls in case of illness or accidents. One homestead in every region has a landing strip where the Royal Flying Doctor Service, which provides the Outback with emergency ambulance transportation, can land its planes. In the Red Center, the mailcarrier is a pilot who flies out with the mail once a week, landing at each ranch to deliver letters, take a cup of tea, and share the news and gossip.

Vehicles are extremely important in the Outback, and it is vital that they be kept in tip-top condition. If someone is badly hurt and must be trucked to a landing strip to meet the flying doctors, a truck that won't start could be fatal. Everybody who drives in the Outback must be a little bit of a mechanic, just as someone at every isolated homestead must be a little bit of a doctor.

When someone leaves a sheep ranch or farm to drive into town, they call first to say they are coming. If they do not arrive and check in by a certain time, the people in town go out looking for them in case there has been an accident or a vehicle has broken down. A breakdown in the desert, particularly in the awful heat of summer, can be fatal. This is why it is common to see cars with extra tires strapped to their roofs, spare fanbelts dangling from the mirrors, and cans of gasoline and drinking water loaded in the back seat.

Many Outback vehicles look like this off-the-road van—packed to the top with emergency equipment.

The Outback is a long, lonely way from the splendid cities on Australia's coastlines, with their rich variety. Yet there are genuine rewards in the Outback, too. There is room to feel free, and to escape from traffic lights and traffic jams.

Making a living in the Outback is hard work. Farming is an uncertain occupation, always at the mercy of the weather. Sheep ranchers work from dawn to dusk in certain seasons, and into the night during shearing. Some

Workers on a sheep ranch in New South Wales are busy shearing the wool from the sheep to sell around the world.

Outback residents mine gleaming opals. Opal mining can be difficult, as workers dig underground, crank pails of soil to the surface one by one, and sift the soil for jewels.

Living in the Outback can also be very profitable. It is not unusual to meet sheep ranchers or farmers who own their own airplanes, send their children to boarding school, and enjoy an occasional vacation in Europe, Fiji, or Singapore. Not all opal miners get rich, but it is not uncommon for one to reach into a jeans pocket and pull out polished gems worth thousands of dollars.

Eat, Drink, and Be Merry!

Because Australians eat everything from potatoes to kangaroos, it would be difficult to say what the national food is. Australia's many immigrants have brought their cooking traditions along with them to their new home. Today, restaurants featuring Chinese, Japanese, Vietnamese, Italian, Greek, and many other types of cooking offer diners great variety in the country's larger, more cosmopolitan cities.

Australia did, however, inherit many dishes and tastes from the English. In the tradition of England, Aussies like sturdy meals. That means they eat a lot of meat, almost always accompanied by potatoes, baked or boiled. Bread is also a staple of most meals. Australians enjoy English meat pies, which consist of meat and gravy in a crust, and are often sold as fast-food items.

Beef is often served as the main course, but equally common is lamb. Every Australian cook, man or woman, can do a thousand things with lamb. One of the most popular dishes, and a delicious one, is curried lamb, usually served as a stew. It is a dish that brings together the Australian national animal, the sheep, with the hot spices of Indonesia and Asia. Australians will carry a pot of curried lamb to a barbecue or a beach party just the way Americans would bring baked beans.

Here is a recipe for lamb curry.

Lamb Curry

2 pounds lamb, any cut, except chops
1 tablespoon vegetable shortening or oil
2 tablespoons curry powder
2 cups beef stock (canned stock or stock made from bouillion cubes may be used)
1/2 cup chopped onion
1/2 cup chopped celery
1 tablespoon chopped fresh parsley

Trim the fat from the meat and then cut the meat into chunks. In a large skillet, brown the meat in the shortening or oil over medium heat. Add the beef stock. Stir in the curry powder. Add the onion, the celery, and the parsley. Stir together. Cover the pan and simmer the mixture for 45 minutes. Serve lamb curry in a large soup bowl with rice or bread.

Some people even eat kangaroos. Those who have say it tastes like veal. It is said to be healthier than beef for humans, since it is not as fatty. But kangaroo isn't cooked too often in Australian kitchens, and only now and then does a restaurant offer it as a novelty. Kangaroo-tail soup, however, is regarded as something of a delicacy and is served in some fine restaurants.

Although meat dishes are still popular, Australians have recently begun to add more fresh vegetables, fruit, and seafood to their diets. Seafood is in fact one of Australia's best offerings. This is understandable since the continent is surrounded by water! Sydney rock oysters, Moreton Bay Bugs (like small crabs), and large crayfish are standard fare.

Barbecues are something of an Australian tradition and so are beach parties. The country's wonderful climate means great weather for outdoor cooking, and its people make the most of it. Both meat and fish are cooked over open fires. A barbecue in the Northern Territory almost certainly would include both barramundi, an enormous fish caught in northern rivers, and steaks of water buffalo, which tastes like beef. Australians imported water buffalo from Indonesia many years ago as beasts of burden. Now they have gone wild, and are hunted for their meat.

Bush picnics and cookouts often serve damper bread and billy tea. Damper is made from wheat flour, mixed with water and then kneaded. The dough is placed on a heavy cast-iron pot that is then put in a hole in the ground and covered with hot coals to bake. Some people wrap it on a stick and cook it over the coals like a toasted marshmallow. Billy tea is prepared in a tin can over the fire.

Some say that the national drink is tea, as it is in England. Others insist that beer is the national favorite. Over twenty-four breweries in Australia produce more than seventy kinds of beer. One of the more famous beers is Foster's Lager in the big can, or "tinny" as the Australians would call it.

Desserts are as popular in Australia as they are everywhere. One treat unique to Australia is a meringue dessert called the pavlova. A square sponge cake covered with chocolate and coconut is called a lamington. A favorite cookie among Australian children is the "AN-ZAC," named for the famous Australian and New Zealand soldiers.

Anzacs

1 cup butter
2 tablespoons maple syrup
1 cup plain flour
1 teaspoon baking powder
1 cup rolled oats
1 cup flaked coconut, unsweetened
1 cup sugar

Soften butter slightly, then cream in with maple syrup. Add the remaining ingredients. Roll into small balls, place well apart on greased baking trays. Bake in moderate oven (350°) for approximately 15 minutes. Cool on tray before removing.

8. *The Australian Classroom*

Australia has as much variety in education as it has in everything else, partly because each Australian state makes its own laws. Since most Australian children live in modern metropolitan areas, they go off to school in the morning and return home in the afternoon just like American children do. But Australian children who live in rural areas of the Outback hardly ever visit a classroom in their early years.

In either case, attendance in school in Australia is required between the ages of six and fifteen, with the exception of the state of Tasmania, where children must attend school until they are sixteen. Kindergarten is not required anywhere, but most children start school earlier than kindergarten anyway. Preschool classes are very popular in Australia, and many children start attending them when they are four years old.

Public Schools

In the United States, we sometimes say that "real school" begins with the first grade. Australians call it "year one." Primary education lasts from year one through year six or seven, depending on the area. The

Children in an Australian classroom take dictation.

emphasis in primary school is on literacy, or teaching every child to read and write. Students also learn simple arithmetic and history. Some schools, but not many, introduce children to foreign languages in primary school. Then secondary school—what we would call high school—begins.

Uniforms are required in practically every Australian school. They are so common that children are used to wearing them. Secondary high schools almost always have dress codes. Although uniforms are not usually required, the dress rules are taken seriously.

Primary schoolchildren usually attend a full day of classes in one classroom, leaving the room only for special activities such as art, music, or gym. Older children, those in their last primary years and those in secondary school, move from classroom to classroom. Some secondary schools are laid out like university campuses. The school day starts at 8:30 A.M. and ends between 3 P.M. and 4 P.M. After-school activities such as sports, band, and drama begin in the late primary years and continue through secondary school.

About 80 percent of all Australian children attend government schools, or public schools. Government schools are free to everyone all the way through secondary school. Non-government schools, either private or religious, charge tuition fees, and are mostly owned and operated by the Roman Catholic church. These schools teach the same basic courses that government schools do. Both public and private school students receive transportation allowances from the government when they have to travel to their schools.

School—at Home!

But the great sheep stations and farms of the Outback are too isolated to permit many country children to

Schoolchildren take a break from school to go on a field trip— by train!

get to the classrooms every day. Even when the children live close enough to be driven to school, the roads may not be reliable. Often the trip is so slow and long that parents decide that the distance is too much for primary schoolchildren.

Outback children usually are taught by their parents at home. Some get their lessons by two-way radio, and some by television. Many take their important examinations by mail.

A radio teacher can talk to many children on different sheep stations and farms at the same time. The teacher can't see the students, so they can come to radio class in their pajamas if their parents don't object. But "two-way" means that the teacher can hear as well as talk, so children have to be prepared for their lessons no matter what they wear. When the teacher asks a question, an answer is expected.

The radio network on which lessons are given is on the same frequency that farmers and ranchers use to pass along emergency messages. Emergency messages have priority over everything. If they come during classes, radio schoolchildren get the same sort of break that city students get when there are surprise fire or tornado drills.

In the Outback, home tutoring is much more common than any other kind of schooling. One of the children's parents is usually the teacher, although when the farm or ranch family can afford it, they sometimes hire a tutor outside the family. Such tutors are usually licensed teachers. Often they are city teachers who want to experience living in the Outback for a while.

Lesson plans for home tutoring are prepared by the government and mailed to Outback homes, so that Outback children will be taught the same courses as students in the cities. Workbooks are required. Once a week or so, pages from the children's workbooks are mailed to town. Here they are checked by school administrators to make sure the right work is being done. Home tutoring is sometimes referred to as correspondence school, and the reason is that the schoolwork is always in the mail.

Depending on the distance, and on the weather and road conditions, Outback children who attend school at home are driven to town at least once a month to spend a day with other children in a regular classroom. This way, children can meet with others of their own age. It also allows them to get used to a classroom. When they reach secondary school age, most Outback children will make the trip to town for classes.

In farm and ranch homes, one room is usually set aside as the children's classroom. The classroom is usually different than the other parts of the house where the children watch TV or just relax. This is meant to help the children understand that education is important to their futures.

A classroom at home might have all the equipment

found in a regular schoolroom, including a blackboard, wall maps, and school desks. These children have a schedule, just like the city schoolchildren do. They report to the classroom after breakfast, go from one subject to another, and break for recess and lunch at the same time every day. The teacher assigns homework and gives tests and quizzes.

Once Outback children reach secondary school age, they usually are sent to the town schools. If they are close enough, they are driven in each day and home again in the evening. If the distance is too far, the children move into town. Some stay in the homes of family friends, others stay in hostels, or supervised lodging, for students. In this case, it becomes the ranch or the farm that the children visit only now and then.

Decision Time

In secondary school, students make important decisions about their futures. With the advice of parents and teachers, each child has to decide what to do. They can learn commercial or technical subjects that outfit a student to find work immediately after high school, or concentrate on college preparatory subjects. This decision is usually made between year ten and eleven. The great majority of Australian high school students choose to concentrate on vocational subjects. They might study agriculture, animal history, or mechanical trades, or they might study for jobs in business offices or the service industries.

In the mid-1980s, there were only nineteen universities in all of Australia. These universities are all publicly owned. There are many more colleges that train people for jobs, such as teaching music or public health nursing.

The universities are almost all located in or near the large cities. Admission to them is based on how well the students did in secondary school. The universities offer a full range of studies, from medicine and law to the humanities. Although a growing number of Australian universities operate graduate schools, students who seek advanced degrees usually go abroad. Most go to England, but many go to other countries in Europe, or to America.

Help for the Students

Australia has special programs for the education of Aborigine children and the children of immigrants for whom English is a second language. In some schools, when Aborigine youngsters report for year one, they will find not only an English-speaking teacher but also an Aborigine teacher's aide who speaks the local tribal dialect. The aide's job is to make the Aborigine children comfortable in the classroom and to help them get used

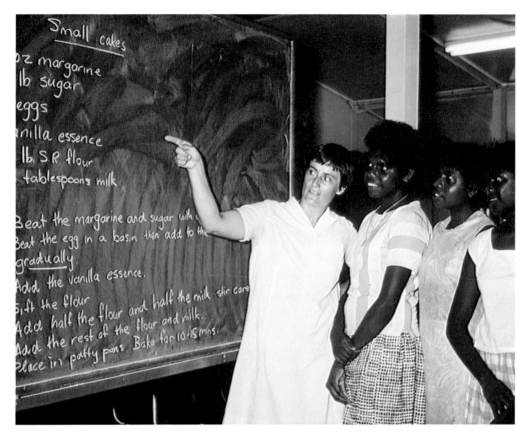

Learning to make small cakes, Aboriginal students take cooking lessons at Koomilda College in Darwin.

to the idea of learning in English. However, an increasing number of students are leaving school as soon as the law allows them to.

New programs are aimed at reducing the high dropout rate of children in secondary school. To encourage Aboriginal students to stay in school, the Australian government often pays their families special allowances to help buy school clothes and other necessities.

Sometimes the programs are unsuccessful. In the 1980s, about two-thirds of all students left school when they were sixteen years old. Because of the determination of the teachers and the help of government educational programs, most of today's Australians can read and write. The children are being taught the importance of education, whether by two-way radio or in the classroom!

9. Sports Under the Sun

When Australia won the America's Cup sailing competition in 1983, the races took place many time zones away in the waters off Newport, Rhode Island. In the past, the Americans were the only ones who had ever won the competition. Back in Australia, there was tremendous excitement. It seems that the entire country stayed up all night to watch the final races on live television.

Prime Minister Bob Hawke went on national television and excused everyone who was late for work or for school the morning after the final race. The America's Cup of 1983 was an exceptional moment. It combined two strong elements of Australian culture: love of country and love of sports.

People all over the world are sports fans and play in every area of the globe. But it is difficult to think of a country that loves sports as much as Australia does.

Almost everyone, young or old, is active in some sport or outdoor activity. Australia's wonderful climate, with its many days of sunshine, makes the country a perfect place for sports. In addition, many workers are entitled to long vacations—four weeks paid for most and six weeks paid for many. This gives them ample free time to devote to their favorite recreation.

Athletes compete in professional matches played in huge stadiums before thousands of spectators and big television audiences, as well as in amateur tournaments played in the tiniest of Outback settlements. Whether the contest is big or small, no one takes the games casually. Australians are serious about their sports, and everyone plays to win.

Cricket and Wickets

Cricket, played in the summer, is perhaps the biggest and most popular sport in Australia. It is also the one closest to the hearts of the people, perhaps because the game comes from England, and has the oldest tradition associated with it. Cricket clubs meet all over Australia. The best players are chosen for the national team, which represents Australia abroad in international matches against England, and other countries that once were part of the British Empire. These international matches, called test matches, are probably the biggest events of the entire Australian sports year. People argue about them months before they happen, and then wait almost in silence for the results.

Some people see a similarity between cricket and baseball. Cricket has a pitcher, called a bowler, and a batter, called a batsman. There are fielders. But there is no "foul" territory. Often the batsman doesn't run after

he hits the ball, and it means nothing if the batsman swings and misses. Instead of pitching the ball the bowler must bounce it to the batsman. Some people think there isn't a lot of resemblance between cricket and baseball after all, if you take a closer look.

Two wickets are set up on the cricket field, one behind the bowler and one behind the batsman. A wicket is made up of three upright wooden sticks, with a wooden slab laid across the top of the sticks. The bowler tries to bounce the ball past the batsman so that the ball, heavier and harder than a baseball, knocks down the wicket. The batsman uses his bat, which is more like a long paddle, to defend the wicket by hitting the ball away.

If the batsman hits the ball far enough, he will run to the bowler's wicket and back to his own. Meanwhile, the fielders try to return the ball and hit the wicket before he can complete his run. If he hits it beyond the field's boundaries, he scores six runs. If he hits the ball into the air and a fielder catches it before it hits the ground, he is out. He is also out if the bowler bounces one past him and knocks down the wicket.

A skilled batsman can bat for more than an hour, and some matches last for days. The traditional "costume" for cricket is white slacks, a white shirt, and white shoes. Each club has caps in its team colors (to go with all that white), and the more colorful the cap the better.

A batsman bats a cricket ball on the greens at a game between Victoria and New South Wales.

Club cricket is often an amateur game. The players hold regular jobs and play cricket on weekends. But the higher a player ranks in competition, the more time the game demands of him. Almost all players on the national teams are professionals who are paid for their sport. And, almost all cricketeers are men, although women's teams play here and there.

Australia's Football

If cricket, so rich in history and tradition, is the first sport in Australia, then rugby runs a very close second. Rugby, called "football" or "footie," is played with a leather ball shaped like an oval. The ball looks a lot like an American football, although it is plumper and has rounder ends. There are eleven or thirteen players on a team, depending on the type of rugby being played, and the object of the game is to carry the ball across a points line, or to score points by aiming accurate kicks between tall upright poles.

As in American football, players tackle and run into each other. However, there are some genuine differences. Rugby is much faster than American football; its players run almost constantly. Games are practically nonstop, with hardly any time-outs called. The players do not wear protective pads or helmets, but the collisions are just as violent.

Rugby, at the top professional level, draws huge crowds. The top players are paid to play, although almost all of them have regular jobs as well. The country also has amateur leagues. Nearly every town, even the very smallest, fields a town team. When the team plays at home, it is an exciting day and almost everyone attends, or so it seems. When the game is held in another town, the team's fans often make the trip in a caravan, even though the journey might take several hours.

Every young boy who plays rugby dreams of someday winning a place on the national team, which plays matches with other countries. It is a great honor for athletes to be asked to represent their countries, especially in Australia, where sports are so popular. Rugby matches are always exciting, but when Australia challenges nearby New Zealand's best players, the fans go wild.

Soccer, Lawn Bowling, and Horse-Racing

Soccer also attracts many followers in Australia, although it ranks behind cricket and rugby in fan interest. Australia is not one of the world's soccer powers yet, but its supporters hope to develop a national team that will become a strong competitor for the World Cup, the highest prize in soccer.

Australia even has professional lawn bowlers and a

Soccer is a popular game throughout Australia—even the tiniest communities have town teams.

national lawn bowling team. In this sport, a white target ball is set in place on a grass court as smooth and slick as a golf putting green. From about twenty-five yards away, the opposing bowlers roll heavy balls, each trying to get closer to the white ball. Lawn bowling is a very quiet game, but like every other game in Australia, competition is keen.

Horse-racing is a gala event in Australia. The Melbourne Cup has become an international classic in thoroughbred racing. The day of the race is a general holiday, with no school and no work, in much of the state of Victoria, and huge crowds gather at the track. But horse-racing is just as exciting in the small towns and cities of the Outback. Practically every town of any size at all has a racetrack and a yearly racing schedule, if only one or two days long.

Many Australians love to gamble, and bookies wearing huge leather purses over their shoulders set up their betting stands on the grass near the track and call the odds. Townspeople get their best clothes out of mothballs and dress up for the races. Almost everybody gets out to the track, which is usually on the outskirts of town, and farmers and ranchers drive in from their lonely spreads. At the small country tracks, fans can lean over the rail and be close enough to the action to feel the thundering hooves of the horses.

Some Famous Aussie Athletes

Australian athletes are best known to Americans through their participation in individual sports such as swimming, track, tennis, and golf. During the 1950s Dawn Fraser held many women's swimming records, and was the swimmer to beat in all her races in the

Olympics. In 1954 Australian runner John Landy pushed Britisher Roger Bannister to the first ever under-four-minutes mile during the Empire Games in Vancouver, Canada.

Australians no longer dominate the world tennis scene. But it was not long ago that Australians Lew Hoad, Rod Laver, Ken Rosewall, and John Newcombe all but ruled men's tennis, and Margaret Court Smith and Evonne Goolagong Cawley took the major women's championships.

Evonne Goolagong Cawley is the part-Aborigine who, at the age of 19, won the tennis championship at Wimbledon, England. Now married and a resident of the United States, she was born in the city of Griffith, 300 miles (480 kilometers) west of Sydney. She grew up in a large family in the town of Barellan, where her father made his living as a mechanic and a sheep shearer.

Perhaps one of the very best golfers in all the world right now is Greg Norman, an Australian raised in Queensland. Norman won the British Open in 1986 and came very close to winning three other major championships. David Graham has won America's National Open. Peter Thomson, now playing the senior professional golf tour in America, won the British Open five times when he was younger. Jan Stephenson, Penny Pulz, and Karen Permezel are three Australian players on the American women's professional golf tour.

Aussie tennis star Evonne Goolagong Cawley.

Sunning, Swimming, and Surfing

Every professional sport played in Australia is played for fun as well. The wonderful climate means people can play year-round. In Sydney, for instance, people say that the weather allows them to swim or sail almost every day. Australians are avid sailors, and every major city on the coast stages competitive regattas, or sailing races. Australian sailors participate in international ocean competitions and, of course, in matches like the America's Cup. In many areas, the waves are high and the surfing is great. There hardly is a weekend when the cities' harbors aren't full of boats of all kinds.

The Australians love to explore the wonders of their country. In the Outback, roaming the wide open spaces is a popular form of recreation. People coming all the way from the coastal cities wander in the great interior in off-the-road vehicles, on horseback, on camels, by light plane, and even by hot-air balloon.

The Great Barrier Reef is a paradise for divers and swimmers, fishermen and sunbathers. Many islands off the reef have been developed as resorts, particularly in the vicinity of Cairns. Some of these islands are so small that there is barely room for a hotel. When the tide is out, vacationers can walk the reef in protective shoes and examine its shapes and colors. There are beaches everywhere, and thousands of tourists visit every year.

An underwater photographer snaps photos of several kinds of coral among the waters of the Great Barrier Reef.

The development of the jet aircraft and then the jumbo jet after World War II has opened up the possibility of easy international travel for Australians, and they take full advantage of the opportunity. Australia is located in an exotic and fascinating part of the world, not far at all from Singapore, Malaysia, Borneo, New Guinea, Fiji, Tahiti, or Bali. Their generous vacation pay helps Australians afford travel to all parts of the world. Australians like nothing better than to be on the go, out of doors, and preferably playing some type of game.

10. Aussies Abroad

Very few Australians have come to America to live. The main reason for this is that Australia is so much like America. Historically, both have offered the same hope of opportunity. They promised their first settlers and the thousands that followed a new chance, room to roam, and new freedoms from old ways.

The one group of Australians that did come to America were the war brides of World War II. Many American soldiers were stationed in Australia during the war, and quite a few romances blossomed between servicemen and Australian women. After the war, the Americans brought their Australian brides with them to the United States. According to best estimates, five thousand to six thousand Australian women came to America at this time.

Though few Americans stayed Down Under after the war, today many Americans are interested in taking up residence in Australia. Australia has become a popular country, partly because of all the attention the country received from the America's Cup yacht race, and from movies such as *Crocodile Dundee*.

Some Americans are finding they do not qualify for emigration to Australia. A list of needed skills is kept by the Australian government, and people who can bring those abilities with them are considered for eventual citizenship. Australian immigration officials watch closely for anyone who merely thinks the living would be easier Down Under, where there are so many generous welfare programs. People with the training and attitude to help Australia progress are the ones who are given the biggest welcome.

Although immigration patterns now run toward Australia, not toward America, the pattern is exactly reversed when it comes to famous Australians. Quite a number of Australians have made international names for themselves in the arts, popular entertainment, sports, politics, publishing, and the sciences. Australia has produced Nobel Prize winners and great stars.

The world-acclaimed opera singer Joan Sutherland is an example of the trend for talented Aussies to leave Australia. Sydney, where her voice was first noticed, is a wonderful place, but the first center of opera is in Europe, and then America. Before she could be known in the way she is today, she had to move to Europe, to sing before the critics and audiences there.

Doctor Helen Caldicott is a respected physician and a specialist in cystic fibrosis, a lung disorder that affects children. But what she is known for internationally is her crusade to rid the world of nuclear weapons. Caldicott came from Australia to the United States to practice

Doctor Helen Caldicott.

medicine at Harvard and because she believes that
America can make a difference in the state of worldwide
nuclear issues. She gives speeches, writes books, films
television programs, and she produced the film *If You
Love This Planet.*

Australia has many fine authors, one of the most
famous being Colleen McCullough. She wrote the inter-

national best-seller *The Thorn Birds.* This book, a grim story about life in the Outback, was later made into a made-for-television movie.

Some popular artists leave Australia to make more money. In Australia's population of over sixteen million, a rock group could possibly sell enough records and tapes to make a very good living. But the chance to strike it rich in America's market is much greater.

Australians don't mind when their stars and heroes leave Down Under for greater acclaim and bigger pay. Australians respect talent and ability, and they understand that theirs is not the world's main stage.

Australian rock groups often become popular in America. The Bee Gees are Australian although they first made it big in Britain. Other Australian rock groups include Air Supply, Midnight Oil, Little River Band, AC/DC, Split Enz, and the Hunters and Collectors. Helen Reddy, the popular singer, went on stage with her family's vaudeville act for the very first time at the age of four in Perth. There are many more Australian musicians, some not yet heard by the wider world.

Aussies do expect a degree of loyalty from the stars who leave Australia. In 1977 when the rock group Air Supply went on a tour with Rod Stewart, Australian fans accused the group of abandoning them for glamour. So in 1982, on Air Supply's second American tour, the group took along stage props to create a backdrop of an

Australian landscape to make the Aussies happy.

Hollywood pays bigger dollars than any other film center in the world, so that is where the best of Australia's movie actors and directors hope to be invited. Sports stars, too, can make more money in America if they succeed.

Peter Weir, who directed *Mosquito Coast, Witness, Gallipoli, Picnic at Hanging Rock,* and *The Year of Living Dangerously,* is Australian. So is Fred Schepisi, who directed *Plenty, Barbarosa,* and *The Chant of Jimmie Blacksmith.*

Paul Hogan, star and screenwriter of *Crocodile Dundee,* which led all films in America in box-office receipts for a number of weeks in late 1986, is as Australian as they come. He was already famous in America for his commercials for Foster's Lager and the Australian Tourist Commission. *Crocodile Dundee,* with its happy-go-lucky hero, its crocodiles and kangaroos, has done wonders for Australian tourism.

Mel Gibson, star of the *Mad Max* movies, *Gallipoli* and *The Year of Living Dangerously,* can be counted among Australians we have all heard of, although he was born in America. He moved to Australia when he was young, and has lived there for most of his life.

The same is true for singer and actress Olivia Newton-John. She was born in England, and moved to Australia when she was five years old. She starred in

Paul Hogan, also known as "Crocodile Dundee," is a great favorite among Americans.

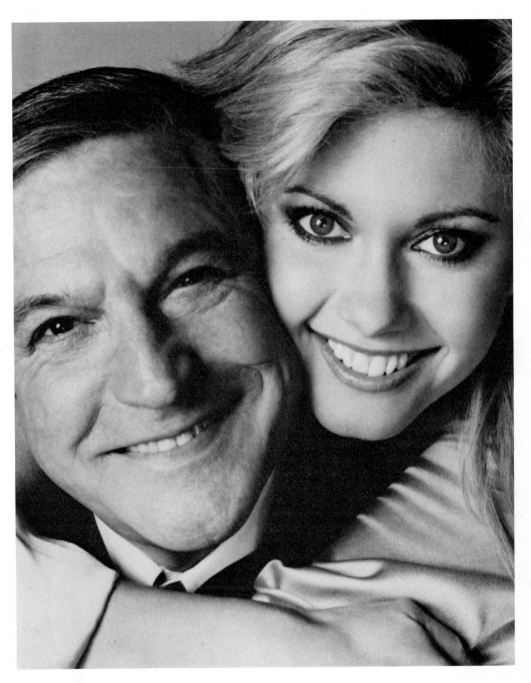

Mel Gibson (left) stars as "Mad Max."

Australian singer and actress Olivia Newton-John (above) hugs her duet partner Gene Kelley in the musical fantasy Xanadu.

Grease with John Travolta, and has more recently appeared in the musical fantasy *Xanadu.*

Though Australians don't mind losing their national
talents to an international arena, they will turn angrily
on a star or a hero who gets a big head. Talent, yes; ego,
no. Stars and heroes are expected to act like plain folks,
without airs, like mates. No one gets dropped quicker
than the star who acts like one.

When an Australian rock star finishes a concert, he
or she can walk out through the crowd without being
mobbed, without anyone making a fuss. People might
call out, "Nice sounds, Mary," or "Good on ya, mates,"
but that's it. Once the show is over, the star is just another
man or woman.

When Joan Sutherland finishes a performance at
the Sydney Opera House, fans always wait for her at the
stage door. When she emerges, she is not surrounded by
bodyguards or by people who specialize in brushing off
the fans. She and her husband, the Australian conductor
Richard Bonynge, walk out together, without help.

They head right over to the waiting fans, and they
chat like they were old friends. They don't hurry, and
stay as long as the fans have something to say. This is
very Australian—relaxed, informal, and friendly. Fan
and star have different talents, but they meet in a way
that says clearly that each person is of value, neither
more important than the other. Much of what is special

about Australia is captured in a moment like this.

As Americans learn more and more about Australia and its wonderful climate and lifestyle, its appeal grows. Many like the general feeling of well-being of Australia. Australia's cities are bright and clean, and life seems quieter and less stressful than life in the fast-paced American society. But Australia's most appealing qualities come from the people themselves. The warmth and sense of humor of the colorful Aussies are truly what make Australia a lucky land.

Appendix A

Australian Slang

English is the language of Australia, and Australians are capable of speaking it just as properly as in the Queen's court of London. But Australia also has a rich slang all its own. Here are some examples:

barby—barbecue.

bikey—a biker.

billy—a tin can (or any other container) that is used to boil water for tea over a fire in the bush. A store-bought steam kettle on the stove in a modern Australian kitchen is also called billy.

bloke—a man. We would say fellow, or guy.

bludger—a sponger, a moocher, or one who lives off others.

bonzer—terrific, as in "That movie is bonzer!" or "She's a bonzer girl!"

bushranger—a bandit or an outlaw.

chook—chicken.

cobber—a friend.

corroboree (koh-ROB-oh-ree)—Aborigine festival.

Crissie—Christmas.

crook—broken, or sick, as in "I'm crook. I think it's the flu," or "My car is crook. I think it's the starter."

cuppa—a cup of tea.

dero—a derelict.

digger—an Australian soldier.

dinkum—genuine, or the real thing. A dinkum hero is one whose heroism cannot be doubted or questioned. "Fair dinkum" means the whole truth.

dunny—outhouse.

flash—showoff, as in "Who's driving that flash car?"

flog—to sell, or hock.
footie—football.
garbo—garbage man.
good on ya!—good for you!
grizzle—to complain.
joey—baby kangaroo still in the pouch.
knackered—tired.
larrikin—tough guy, or hoodlum.
mate—your best buddy, your comrade. Not your spouse.
mossie (or mozzie)—mosquito.
nick—steal.
nit—fool.
ocker—bumpkin, or loudmouth.
postie—postman.
roo—kangaroo.
salvo—member of the Salvation Army.
she'll be apples—it will be all right.
silvertail—member of high society.
slats—ribs.
snags—sausages.
stickybeak—busybody.
too right!—exactly!
uni—university.
walkabout—to wander. This term comes from the early days
    when men who tired of a job or a place would put their
    belongings on their backs and set off on foot. They were said
    to have gone walkabout.
walloper—policeman.
wowser—a killjoy, or party-pooper.

Appendix B

Consulates and Embassies in the United States and Canada

Australian Consulates in the United States and Canada offer assistance and resource information to Americans and Canadians who want to learn more about Australia.

U.S. Embassy and Consulates

Washington, D.C.
Embassy of Australia
1601 Massachusetts Avenue Northwest
Washington, D.C. 20036
Phone (202) 797-3000

Chicago, Illinois
Consulate General of Australia
321 North Clark Street, Suite 2930
Chicago, Illinois 60610
Phone (312) 645-9440

Honolulu, Hawaii
Consulate General of Australia
1000 Bishop Street
Honolulu, Hawaii 96813
Phone (808) 524-5050

Houston, Texas
Consulate General of Australia
1990 Post Oak Road
Houston, Texas 77056
Phone (713) 629-9131

Los Angeles, California
Consulate General of Australia
3550 Wilshire Boulevard
Los Angeles, California 90010
Phone (213) 380-0980

New York, New York
Consulate General of Australia
636 Fifth Avenue
New York, New York 10020
Phone (212) 245-4013

San Francisco, California
Consulate General of Australia
360 Post
San Francisco, California 95113
Phone (415) 362-6160

Canadian Embassy and Consulates

Ottawa, Ontario
Office of the High Commissioner
130 Slater Street
Ottawa, Ontario K1P6E2
Phone (613) 236-0841

Toronto, Ontario
Consulate General of Australia
2200 Commerce Center
P. O. Box 69
King and Bay Streets
Toronto, Ontario M5C169
Phone (416) 367-0783

Vancouver, British Columbia
Consulate General of Australia
1066 West Hastings
Vancouver, British Columbia
V633X1
Phone (604) 684-1177

Australia also maintains a mission at the United Nations, and has tourism offices in New York, Los Angeles, and Toronto.

United Nations
1 Dag Hammarskjold Plaza
New York, New York 10017

Selected Bibliography

Bernardi, Debra, ed. *Fodor's Australia, New Zealand, and the South Pacific.* New York: Fodor's Modern Guides, 1987.

Clifton, T. "The Laid-Back and Lucky Land." *Newsweek* (February 2, 1987):38-39.

Christmas, Linda. *The Ribbon and the Ragged Square: An Australian Journey.* Middlesex: Penguin Books, Ltd, 1986.

Ellis, Rennie. *We Live in Australia.* New York: Bookwright Press, 1983.

Fry, Eric, ed. *Rebels and Radicals.* Boston: George Allen & Unwin, 1983.

Horne, Donald. *The Australian People: Biography of a Nation.* London: Angus and Robertson (Publishers) Pty Ltd, 1972.

Lepthien, Emilie U. *Australia.* Chicago: Children's Press, 1982.

Mudie, Ian. *Australia Today.* London: Kaye & Ward Ltd., in association with Hicks, Smith & Sons, Australia and New Zealand, 1974.

Ritchie, John. *Australia As Once We Were.* New York: Holmes & Meier Publishers, Inc., 1975.

Shaw, A.G.L., *The Story of Australia.* Fifth edition, revised. Boston: Faber and Faber, 1983.

Ward, Russel. *The History of Australia: The Twentieth Century.* New York: Harper & Row, 1977.

Index

Aborigines: art of, 44, 78; festivals of, 88-89; national character and, 30; number of, 41, 42; origin of, 17, 42-44, 76; problems of, 28-29; in school, 119; white settlers and, 39, 50-53, 56
Adelaide, 14-15, 23-24, 55-56, 93
Alice Springs, 86, 93
America's Cup, 14, 24, 79, 122, 132, 134
Antarctica, 25, 45
anthem, 62
ANZAC (Australian and New Zealand Army Corps), 62-64
ANZUS Treaty, 65-66
Asia, 24, 39, 42, 64, 69
Australian Capital Territory, 14, 25
Australian Alps, 15
Ayers Rock, 16, 43

Bass, George, 54
Bathurst, 36, 59-60
Bathurst Island, 56
birds, 78-80
Blue Mountains, 23, 55
Boer Wars, 62, 85
Botany Bay, 48-50
Brisbane, 14-15, 26, 93
Burke, Robert O'Hara, 58
bushrangers, 32, 36

Caldicott, Dr. Helen, 135-136
camels, 57, 86
Canberra, 14, 25
Cape York Peninsula, 46, 48
Cawley, Evonne Goolagong, 130
Commonwealth, 86
convicts, 30, 49, 53

Cook, Captain James, 47-49
Crocodile Dundee, 134, 138
crocodiles, 77

Dampier, William, 46-47
Darling River, 24
Darwin, 14, 24-25, 65, 76
dingo, 76
discovery, 45, 54

echidna, 75-76
economy, 20-21, 29, 57-58, 63-65, 67-68
emu, 78
entertainment, 99, 101, 137
Eyre, Edward John, 58

Fiji, 46, 106, 133
First Fleet, 50, 83
Flinders, Matthew, 54
flowers, 80, 82
foods, 107-110
Fraser, Dawn, 129-130

galahs, 79-80
Gallipoli Peninsula, 62
geography, 10, 14-16, 19, 26, 69
Gibson Desert, 18
Gibson, Mel, 138
gold, 20, 36, 59-60
government, 11-12, 14, 61-62, 85
Graham, David, 130
Great Barrier Reef, 26, 130
"Great Empty," 19, 101
Great Sandy Desert, 18
Great Victoria Desert, 18
Griffin, Walter Burley, 25

Hawke, Robert (Bob), 12, 122
Hobart, 14, 25
Hogan, Paul, 138
holidays: Adelaide Cup Day, 86; ANZAC Day, 84-85; Australia Day, 50, 83-84; Boxing Day, 90, 92; Chinese New Year's, 87; Christmas, 83, 89-90; Commonwealth Day, 85; corroboree, 88-89; Easter, 83, 92; ethnic, 87-88; Labor Day, 86; Melbourne Cup Day, 86, 129; New Year's Day, 83, 92
housing, 96-99

immigration, 28, 67, 86, 137
Indian Ocean, 10, 24, 56
Indonesia, 24

Jansz, Willem, 46, 48

kangaroos, 21, 68, 69, 71-72, 75, 78, 108-109
Kelly, Ned, 36-37
koala, 21, 69, 72, 74-75
Kookaburra, 79
kookaburra, 79

labor unions, 37-38
Lachlan River, 55
Lake Alexandria, 55
Lake Disappointment, 19
Landy, John, 130
language, 32
lily walker, 78-79
lizards: frill-necked, 77; goanna, 76; monitor, 76
MacArthur, John, 57
McCullough, Colleen, 137
MacDonnell Range, 15-16

Macquarie, Lachlan, 54-55
Macquarie River, 36
marsupials, 69, 71, 74
Melbourne, 14, 23, 25, 56, 60, 80
Melville Island, 56
Mount Kosciusko, 15
Murray River, 23-24, 55
Murrumbidgee River, 55
Musgrave Range, 15

national character, 9, 30-31, 39, 41, 143
New Guinea, 42, 45, 85, 133
New South Wales, 12, 14, 20, 24, 50, 54-55, 61
Newton-John, Olivia, 138, 142
New Zealand, 46, 65-66, 68, 110, 127
Norman, Greg, 130
Northern Territory, 14, 20, 24, 77
nuclear politics, 66, 135-136
nuclear weapons, 20, 66, 135-136

Outback: Aborigines and, 41, 89; birds of, 80; code of, 34; economy of, 22; family life in, 102; 104-105, 137; geography of, 16-19; houses in, 101; mining in, 20, 106-107; national character and, 31, 93; recreation and, 132; settlers of, 34; sports in, 86, 123, 129; work in, 34, 36, 38

Parramatta, 55
penguins, 80
Perth, 14, 24, 56, 79, 137
Phillip, Captain Arthur, 49-50, 83
Phillip Island, 80
platypus, 75-76
population, 10, 15, 28, 66-67
Port Phillip, 56

prison (penal) colony, 48-49

Queen Elizabeth II, 11, 86
Queensland, 14, 20, 25, 26, 61, 77, 130
Queen Victoria, 61

recipes, 108, 110
Red Center, 18, 57, 104
religion, 11
Royal Perth Yacht Club, 24

Schepisi, Fred, 138
schools: Aborigines in, 119-120; daily schedule
    of, 114; government allowances and, 120-
    121; in Outback, 114, 116-118; primary, 112-
    114; secondary, 113-114, 118; types of, 114;
    uniforms in, 113-114; universities, 119
Second Fleet, 53
settlers, 11, 39, 42-44, 50-56, 84
sheep, merino, 21-22, 57
sheep ranchers, 31, 34, 105, 106
Simpson Desert, 18
size, 10
slang, 18, 32
Smith, Margaret Court, 130
Snowy Mountains, 15, 24
South Australia, 12, 14, 20, 61
Southeast Asia, 28, 42, 67, 76
sports: climate and, 122, 132; cricket, 123, 125-
    126; diving, 132; horse-racing, 129; lawn
    bowling, 127-128; Melbourne Cup, 129; in
    Outback, 123; rugby, 126-127; sailing, 132;
    soccer, 127; swimming, 132
squatters, 57
states, 12, 14
Stirling, Captain James, 56

Sturt, Charles, 55-56, 59
Sutherland, Joan, 135, 142
swagmen, 31, 32-35, 37, 68
Swan River, 56
Sydney: economy of, 22; farming in, 55; as
    federal capital, 25; foods in, 99-101; found-
    ing of, 50; geography of, 23, 93, 96-97; gold
    and, 36, 59-60; government of, 50, 53; nam-
    ing of, 50; population of, 23
Sydney Harbor (Port Jackson), 50, 55, 83, 96
Sydney Opera House, 23, 99, 142
Sydney, Viscount, 50
symbol, 71

Tasman, Abel, 46
Tasmania, 14, 25, 46, 50, 61
Tasman Sea, 46
Terra Australis Incognita, 45, 48, 55
Thompson, Peter, 130
Torres, Luis Vaez de, 45-46
"transportation," 49, 53, 61
trees, 80, 82

United Nations, 65

Victoria, 12, 14, 61

"Waltzing Matilda," 33
Weir, Peter, 138
Western Australia, 12, 20, 56, 61
wombat, 74-75
World War I, 62-63
World War II, 12, 28, 30, 39, 63-65, 85, 134

About the Author

Al Stark is a writer for the *Detroit News*, Detroit, Michigan, and the father of six children. He is the author of another of the Discovering Our Heritage books published by Dillon Press, *Zimbabwe: A Treasure of Africa*, published in 1986.

Stark traveled to Australia for the *Detroit News* in 1986. He wrote a series of feature articles on Australia in advance of the America's Cup sailing races. Stark's daughter, Allana, accompanied him on his trip to Australia, and helped him with this book.